Best wishes
to Aunt & Dorothy

Bruce

Stategies in counseling
for behavior change

Century Psychology Series

Kenneth MacCorquodale,
Gardner Lindzey, and Kenneth E. Clark
Editors

STRATEGIES IN COUNSELING
FOR BEHAVIOR CHANGE

Samuel H. Osipow & W. Bruce Walsh
BOTH OF THE OHIO STATE UNIVERSITY

APPLETON-CENTURY-CROFTS
EDUCATIONAL DIVISION

New York MEREDITH CORPORATION

PRINTED IN THE UNITED STATES OF AMERICA

390–68332–9

To Our Parents

Preface

This book was written in a social climate characterized by a demand for action and change. It is our hope that the flavor of change permeates this book. In order to make a significant social contribution counseling psychology must take more initiative in planning and promoting change. Counseling must develop the concepts and the means to help people bring their lives as much under their own control as possible. To do this, counselors must accept greater responsibility than heretofore, and not insist that clients take the lion's share of responsibility for change.

We think our work here represents one aspect of a growing sense of awareness among counselors that counseling objectives must be raised from the level of concern primarily with helping people *feel* better to encompass promoting growth in both feeling *and* action.

We have come to this view by different routes, but we have both been influenced by many others along our various ways. These people are too numerous to acknowledge individually, but it should be noted that they include both our colleagues and our clients. We wish to acknowledge the specific help in the preparation of this volume of Robert E. Campbell, Sondra F. Osipow, and the members of the Seminar in Behavioral Approaches to Counseling held in the fall of 1968 in the Department of Psychology at the Ohio State University. Though they influenced us, we alone are responsible for the failings and flaws this book possesses. We hope the weaknesses will impell others to correct them.

S.H.O. *and* W.B.W.

Contents

PART 1

Chapter 1

Theoretical Foundations

This work has as its objective the integration of several existing approaches to counseling in the hope that the counselor will be able to apply current theory and method more effectively. Ideally, the counselor should develop distinctive strategies, each likely to be particularly effective in working with a special type of the many human problems, concerns, and decisions that are presented.

The question of the role of theoretical foundations for counseling has been discussed and debated voluminously. These debates have centered about two major issues. The first issue concerns the particular usefulness of theory in general for the counselor. In what way is the practitioner able to perform his service more effectively if he has a set of guiding theoretical principles? The second issue concerns the question of whether an adequate theoretical formulation for counseling exists and, if so, which of the many theoretical proposals has the most to offer the counselor?

The first question may appropriately be rephrased by asking what distinctive value lies in counseling from an integrated theoretical point of view that does not exist for the counselor who draws separately upon the formulations of learning theory, personality theory, and measurement theory. In answer, it is possible to identify four ways in which a counseling theory can help. These are first, the role that may be played by theory in facilitating counselor planning of strategies; second, theory's contribution toward the understanding of individual behavior; thirdly, the suggestions regarding counseling procedures that theory generates; and finally, the guidelines it sets for objectives and the evaluation of counseling activities and outcomes (Ford and Urban, 1963; Stefflre, 1965; Osipow, 1968).

What is the basis for the choice of behavior that a counselor engages in at the very outset of his efforts? What leads the psychoanalyst to have his patient lie on a couch looking away from the therapist, and free-associate (indeed what leads him to refer to himself as a therapist and the object of

3

his attention as a patient?) in contrast to the counselor who seats the client across the desk from himself and takes a case history? What variables lead the counselor to make the particular opening response he chooses? Counselors obviously have different modes of approach to their work, and these differing approaches are in large part dictated by their understandings and predictions about human events. To the extent that these understandings are explicit and formal, and in common with those of other groups of professionals, a counselor may be said to be operating from a systematic point of view; to the extent that many counselors do so, they are likely to increase the consistency which may be observed in their counseling efforts.

Theory also provides the counselor with a framework within which to organize his observations of human beings. An effective theory will be explicit enough to suggest to him aspects of the client behavior which are not immediately observable, to be used in a way similar to the cues that one gets from the shape and surrounding coloration of an empty space in a jigsaw puzzle. For example, a theory which leads to explicit statements about the etiology of a class of choice problems in general can provide a counselor with unusual insight into a particular individual's choice problem. Thus, witness the counselor whose theory tells him that choice problems represent mild obsessional difficulties, and that mild obsessional difficulties stem from a fear of engaging in risk, taking activities. Such a formulation would provide the counselor with a large set of specific behaviors to investigate in order to validate his theoretically derived hypothesis, as well as leading him to understand the broader implications of the client's complaint.

A third contribution of theory to the counseling function is in the realm of counseling technique. What is important for the counselor to do and what should he avoid? Even theories which purport to minimize counselor technique, such as the client-centered view, stress certain counselor behaviors and attitudes as being essential to counselor effectiveness and cite others as inimical to progress. Theory relates concepts about human behavior to the actions of counselors with respect to their clients to events that occur both in and out of interviews. A counselor whose theory emphasizes the cognitive aspects of human behavior employs rational, persuasive techniques. He explains the connection of behaviors and their outcomes to his client, encourages the client to explore his effectiveness in employing certain kinds of behaviors, verbally reinforces successes the client has, and in general, tries to help the client solve his problem logically or make his decision systematically. On the other hand, the counselor whose theory is essentially concerned with emotional aspects of life is likely to focus on the feelings generated between the client and counselor in the counseling interview with the expectation that when the emotional difficulties of the client are resolved in the counseling setting, the resolution will generalize to the larger world.

Finally, both the selection of counseling objectives and identification of methods to evaluate the effectiveness of obtaining these objectives, are within the province of theory's contribution to the counseling task. Suggestions about which behaviors might appropriately be changed to bring about the client's desired end stem from theory. What goals are appropriate for the client who needs to make an educational decision, but for some reason cannot? Obviously, the goal is for him to make the necessary decision, but certain subgoals along the way must be identified and these will vary according to one's theoretical orientation. One counselor might conceive of the ability to make decisions as a function of the possession of relevant information, and thus, his counseling efforts are first aimed toward identifying the information the client possesses and what information he needs, but lacks. Secondly, his efforts go toward providing the information, and seeing to it that the client understands and can use information in making his decision. Another counselor might view such a difficulty as a manifestation of a fear of failure pattern and consequently focus his counseling on eliciting the inappropriate aspects from the client and trying to modify them, with the objective of having the client engage in more risk-taking situations after counseling than formerly. In addition, one counselor might specify behaviorally those events he wishes to bring about. It can be seen that theories vary in the degree to which they aim at the formulation of explicit goals and behaviors, as well as in the kind of goals and behaviors they seek to augment.

The question of the superiority of one counseling theory over another is a more difficult question to respond to than the first. Counseling theories currently exist at varying levels of maturity and possess different objectives. Patterson (1966) has organized counseling theories into five categories, according to their different emphases: rational, learning, analytic, perceptual, and existential. Let us examine some of the major points of difference that exist with respect to theories so categorized.

Rational theories. These theories have as their basis the assumption that man is fundamentally logical in nature, and that given the proper conditions, his intellectual capabilities will enable him to solve his problems effectively, make appropriate decisions, and develop the potential of his capabilities fully. They assume that man is a self-actualizing "being" but that this development can occur positively or negatively. In counseling, the rational view is represented by the theories of Williamson (1950) and Ellis (1962). In attempting to accomplish the goals described above, the counselor plays the role of teacher-collaborator. He is an expert to whom the client comes for consultation, yet the counselor does not take complete control of the client's life, but, instead engages in a joint decision-making process initially in order to identify objectives. The interchange is mainly cognitive in nature, cognitive in the sense that the focus is on the identification of intellectual problem solving behaviors as opposed to subjective emotional responses.

For Williamson, the consultative process occurs verbally and follows a clear sequence. Analysis, the first stage, is a data collection task. Synthesis is the stage where the data are collated. During diagnosis the collated data are scrutinized for patterns and sequences of behavior that may be of critical importance to the client situation. Finally, counseling is where the application of the three previous steps is made to enable the client to solve his problem or make and implement a decision.

To Ellis the process is similar, though with slightly different emphasis. Ellis' clientele is likely to be more disordered psychologically than Williamson's; so Ellis naturally focuses more on the identification of illogical thought sequences and ways to modify them than does Williamson. In this interchange, the counselor identifies the illogical sequences for the client, shows him how they are disrupted in general, specifies the particular sequences concerned, and teaches the client how to "rethink" or "reinterpret" events more logically. The counselor may be more a counter-propagandist than a teacher-collaborator, but elements of the latter remain. Considerable effort may be directed toward getting the client to engage in some form of the feared behavior.

For both Williamson and Ellis, a major objective is change in behavior outside of the interview situation. Williamson's technique was developed and applied in an academic setting where behavior pathology is minimal and where clients possess greater than average intellectual resources and, in fact, may be more than usually accustomed to solving problems and making decisions on the basis of reasoning and intellectual effort. Ellis' efforts notwithstanding, the techniques of the rational school are not likely to be effective with seriously disordered individuals or those with marginal intellectual resources, because these people are less able to bring to bear the behaviors necessary for the rational process to be effective.

Learning approaches. In general, the learning theory approaches are based on principles about human learning, or some part of the large body of empirical data concerning learning. These views are oriented toward problem solving; that is, the development of some skill which will enable the client to be more effective or the elimination of some undesirable response sequence. These theories may be oriented to larger response sequences, such as Dollard and Miller's (1950) work, or they may be aimed at changing highly specific and limited sets of responses, such as are illustrated by the work of Wolpe (1958) and elaborated by others (e.g. Phillips and Wiener, 1966). Or, the learning approaches may be based upon the principles of respondent or operant conditioning. What these views do share is their relative emphasis on overt behavior rather than subjective responses of clients. Behavior problems are viewed as patterns of inappropriate responses possibly learned in connection with aversive stimulus conditions and maintained because of their effectiveness in assisting in the avoidance of undesirable consequences. A major task of the counselor is to help the client learn that the original learning conditions have been (or can be) changed so that the undesirable responses are no longer necessary for the avoidance of the anticipated unpleasant consequence. Thus, clients learn that it may not be necessary to engage in obsessive thinking in order to avoid guilt-producing thoughts.

Another major counselor task stemming from the learning view is helping the client identify and specify aspects of his behavior that may potentially fall under his direct control. This is in sharp contrast to the mental health view of problem behavior which sees mental distress as a reflection of a central disturbance (in other words, based on the disease model of medicine to be discussed in detail in Chapter 2). The behavior based viewpoint leads to treatment conducted by psychologically rather than psychiatrically-oriented practitioners and focuses on goals such as symptom removal *per se* instead of the resolution of problem behavior through the identification of *dynamic* causes. By symptomatic goals is meant the removal of the specific complaints and problems of the client. By nature, then, the learning approaches are not historical in the analytic sesnse, but they do require case history data in the form of information about conditions surrounding the original learning.

The learning views approach the task of behavior change from a variety of directions. Wolpe (1958), for example, introduces the idea of teaching or eliciting from the client a response which is incompatible with and stronger than the undesirable response, thereby eliminating the undesirable response as a problem since it no longer occurs. For example, a strong sexual stimulus might lead to a sequence of sexual responses which interfere with and short circuit an anxiety pattern. Or the technique might present the anxiety pro-voking stimuli thus eliciting the anxious response, at the same time presenting the client with the possibility of engaging in a set of incompatible responses such as self-assertion. A client might first be taught to relax in the anxiety-producing situation through a systematic exposure procedure. Once a predetermined level of relaxation was reached, the counselor using this approach would elicit small, but increasingly assertive, responses to the feared stimuli. Presumably, a point will eventually be reached where the client can control his anxiety responses by countering them with the newly acquired and stronger assertive behaviors.

The learning approach of Rotter (1954) is similar, but less specific. The goal is to lead the client to emit the desired behavior and be rewarded, or failing the possibility of his engaging in the desired behavior directly, to increase the probability of the client's emission of behavior by changing his expectancies about the outcome of the behavior. Similarly, Dollard and Miller (1950), and Pepinsky and Pepinsky (1954) emphasized the client's ability to discriminate among the events surrounding his anxiety arousal, followed by the acquisition of new ways of responding, first in the interview setting, eventually in the natural setting.

In summary, the learning approaches share several features. They work toward identification of the behavior to be modified, the identification of the conditions under which the behavior occurs, the identification of the factors maintaining the behavior, the arrangement of appropriate learning conditions, and the development of a suitable retraining schedule.

Psychoanalytic views. This conception of man sees him as caught in a lifelong struggle between his natural hedonistic, self-gratifying impulses on the one hand and his socially based, self-effacing responses on the other. Accordingly, man's natural impulses conflict with society's expectations of him creating behaviors representative of anxiety and distress in a variety of forms. This distress characteristically is seen to take one or a combination of several forms. Very commonly, socially unacceptable urges are repressed to the unconscious level. The energy so covered up may emerge in the troubled individual in the form of psychogenic physical complaints, pathological anxiety or depression. In the less severely troubled person, various defenses such as rationalization, may be observed. Still other people may find socially acceptable ways to release their libidinal psychic energies (sublimation).

The task of the therapist (or psychoanalytically-oriented counselor such as Bordin, 1968) is to focus upon the specific underlying causes of the conflict within an individual and interpret the meaning of his behavior to the patient, with the objective of making unconscious motives conscious. The ultimate hope is to enable the patient to develop more acceptable social ways of dealing with the tensions created by his conflicts. In medically oriented analysis the techniques commonly used are free association, interpretation, and features that devolve upon the therapist as a result of transference and counter-transference relationships. In counseling settings, where clients are less disturbed, the methods are more likely to concentrate on the interpretations of the client's defenses to him as these defenses serve the interests of the ego.

Perceptual-phenomenological views. These viewpoints have had a major impact on the nature of counseling as it exists today mainly through the writings of Carl Rogers (1942; 1951), though the writings of George Kelly (1955) fall within the general framework of perceptual phenomenological theory. This approach emphasizes the need of a counselor to know the client's frame of reference, though the reason for this need to know is not the same for all theorists. For Rogers, it is with the aim of facilitating the development of healthy impulses within the individual. For Kelly, understanding the client's phenomenological world is necessary to help the client revise his personal constructs about the world. This revision is accomplished through the counselor's efforts to accelerate the tempo of the client's experience, foster his experimentation with new behaviors, enable the client to bring old events and interpretations of those events up-to-date, serve as a source against which he can validate experiences and perceptions, and serve as a vehicle adding new conceptual elements to the client's phenomenal field.

From Rogers' point of view, the need to enter a client's frame of reference completely stems from the postulate that in so doing the counselor can empathize most effectively and genuinely share the client's feelings. The total acceptance of the client that results, frees him from the fear of negative social evaluation which inhibits and constricts his ability to respond spontaneously, openly, and positively to his environment. While it is not technique centered, the client-centered point of view of Rogers is best served by means of techniques which lead to counselor understanding of client affect and the communication of this understanding to the client, along with complete counselor acceptance of the client as a human being, without thought to evaluation of his behavior from a moral or efficiency standard.

Existential views. Of all the views of counseling, the existential is most difficult to characterize. However, it is possible to identify four common areas of attention. One concerns the existential emphasis on the significance of human awareness and self-consciousness. A second is the importance given to the individual's recognition of his ability to influence events concerning himself. A third common element is the importance seen in the integration of the self with the environment. Finally, these views emphasize the role that man's awareness of his eventual death and the anxiety that results from this awareness plays in the shaping of human affairs.

It must be noted that the existential views related to counseling and psychotherapy are not the nihilistic views often associated with existential philosophy. To some extent, the rational views, and, more obviously the perceptual-phenomenal viewpoints, share elements of existential thought. The difference seems to lie in the existentialists' great concern for individual subjective feelings, while the other approaches to counseling are, to varying degrees, committed to changes in behavior growing out of changes in subjective responses.

The existentially oriented counseling theories strive to foster the individual's experiencing of his world and to increase his commitment to life primarily by means of focusing on his immediate present. In general, however, the techniques used by existential counselors are as varied as the number of counselors following the existential approach. The existential point of view concerning the counseling task is illustrated by the work of Frankl (1962) and Kaam (1967).

COUNSELING DEFINITIONS

Differences in definitions of counseling are evident throughout the literature. The variability is, in some degree, the result of differences among counselors with regard to basic philosophy. The early traditional definitions of counseling (Wrenn, 1951; Shostrom and Brammer, 1952) focused on the counseling relationship. Gustad (1953) changed the orientation slightly by emphasizing the learning involved in counseling. Wolberg (1954) added the dimension of concern with the counseling outcome. Others (Bordin, 1955; Division of Counseling Psychology, 1956 and 1961; Patterson, 1967; Pepinsky and Pepinsky, 1954; Perez, 1965; Stefflre, 1965; Tyler, 1961) have presented definitions which combine process, relationship, and outcome in a variety of ways. In general, traditionally oriented counselors have given a minimum of emphasis to making the definitions operational, thus limiting their usefulness.

An alternative to the process-relationship view of counseling involves a developmental orientation. Attempts to define counseling from a developmental frame of reference have been surprisingly few in number. Oetting (1967) sees counseling psychology as the study of the mental health of individuals in the developmental process. Mental health is seen as the ability of a person to engage in and use developmental tasks to further his own personal development. In Oetting's framework, a mental health problem prevents or interferes with an individual's ability to engage in developmental tasks for personal growth.

In a similar vein, Blocher (1966) sees the objective of counseling to be the maximization of a client's freedom to develop within individual and environmental limitations. In this sense, developmental counseling can foster the client's self-awareness of and knowledge about, his reactions to his environment. In general, the developmental definitions focus on the individual's personal growth and maturation, but, are only slightly more operational than traditional definitions of counseling.

Existential definitions of counseling and psychotherapy generally are concerned with understanding the client as he exists in his world. English and English (1958) have defined existential analysis as a method of therapy designed to assist a person to react spontaneously to the world in a spirit of free will. Kaam (1967) sees counseling primarily as a human encounter, where encounter entails sharing the life and existence of the other person. Arbuckle (1965) defines counseling in terms of a human relationship in which the client is to grow and develop his capacities. In general, the existential definitions see counseling as the subjective encounter of two individuals in an affective relationship. There is concern for the understanding of the individual as he exists in his own world. The individual is seen as an emerging, becoming, and existing entity whose person is to be enhanced by the counseling effort. Obviously, the existential views are antagonistic to operational analysis.

Counseling: A definition

In this book, a behavioral and developmental approach is emphasized. Counseling is seen as an attempt to facilitate the learning process by focusing on the relationship between the individual's overt responses (both instrumental and mediational) (Dollard and Miller, 1950) and his environment in order to aid the development process and broaden the individual's problem solving and coping response repertoire.

Counseling, in facilitating the learning process, attempts to help the individual acquire and accumulate significant responses that he may implement under differential conditions. Ideally, the implementation of responses acquired through this process will move the individual toward personal effectiveness and, therefore, facilitate the developmental process. The developmental process is a progressive change leading to a higher degree of differentiation. The process consists of physiological, social, emotional, intellectual, and vocational change.

The behavioral data used to facilitate the learning process in this frame of reference are instrumental and mediational in nature. Overt responses are labeled instrumental. The instrumental response has an immediate effect upon the environment. Further, an instrumental response may be either cognitive or affective in nature. The cognitive instrumental response is purposeful and goal directed overt behavior. The affective instrumental response is emotional and feeling oriented behavior, whose effect on the environment is likely to be more diffuse than the cognitive instrumental response.

Mediational responses have no direct effect upon the environment but lead the way to an instrumental response sequence. Therefore, an overt mediating response can probably be related to an instrumental response sequence and hence become meaningful behavioral data. However, subjective mediational responses, for example, thinking responses, cannot be labeled meaningful behavioral data to an outsider until verbalized or otherwise made accessible. Much of the task of a counselor is aimed at eliciting the subjective mediating responses, thus making them accessible to outside observation, evaluation and change. Mediational responses, of course, may be either cognitive or affective in nature.

The response sequence begins with mediating responses of either the cognitive or affective variety, which lead to the selection and manifestation of a series of instrumental responses. Mediating responses are interspersed with instrumental responses, since the mediating responses provide continual guidelines for the choice of instrumental responses.

Previously, it was suggested that counseling facilitates the learning process by helping the individual acquire significant experiences and responses that may be implemented under differential conditions. This accumulation of experiences and responses is called a repertoire. The repertoire of problem solving and coping responses possessed by the individual aids him in problem solving by identifying desired goals and means to achieve them. Previous experiences and responses of the individual help him make judgments about and engage in behaviors leading to the completion of tasks. In coping, the individual is able to use and conceptually manipulate previous experiences and responses in order to contend with different stimuli under new conditions. In general, in both problem solving and coping, the individual uses the learning process to effect the developmental process in a positive manner.

Behavioral background

The behavioral conceptions of counseling build upon the views of B. F. Skinner. To Skinner (1953) the attention of other people is reinforcing because it is a necessary condition for receiving other, more specific, reinforcements from them. In general, only those people who are attending to us reinforce our behavior. One of these views (Krasner, 1962) calls the therapist a "social reinforcement machine". Krasner assumes that psychotherapy is a lawful, predictable, and directive process which can be investigated most parsimoniously within the framework of a reinforcement theory of learning. A second assumption is that the variables which affect the therapy process are the same as those affecting other interpersonal situations which involve the reinforcement, control, manipulation, influencing, or redirection of human behavior. Thus, Krasner considers a major problem for the counselor to be the identification of the conditions under which the reinforcement procedure is most effective in producing desired behavior changes.

Ullmann and Krasner (1965) closely follow the work of Robert Watson (1962), who wrote that behavior modification includes a variety of techniques, all broadly related to the field of learning, but emphasizes learning with a specific objective, namely, clinical treatment and behavior change. To Ullmann and Krasner this definition is important in two ways. First, the basis of treatment stems from learning theory, which deals with the effect of experience on behavior. Second, behavior modification is based on a body of experimental work dealing with the relationship between changes in the environment and changes in the subject's responses.

Ullmann and Krasner (1965) suggest that the behavior therapist is likely to ask three questions: (a) what subject behaviors should be increased or decreased? (b) what environmental contingencies currently support the subject's behavior? and (c) what environmental changes, ordinarily reinforcers, may be manipulated to alter the subject's behavior favorably? In a similar vein, Phillips and Wiener (1966) refer to the counselor or therapist as an "architect of change" who is willing to design or plan for behavioral modification, using all reasonable resources available to him in specific structured ways. Phillips and Wiener perceive the therapist to be one who applies the principles of behavior theory or cybernetics[1] to develop responses

1. Cybernetics is generally considered to be the study of control and communication in human beings and in machines (Wiener, 1948).

or action directed toward the solution of specific individual and social problems. The "architect" becomes a strategist in the design of new behaviors and solving behavior problems.

Following the same kind of reasoning, Krumboltz (1966b) expressed the idea that counselors should conceive of client problems as problems in learning. According to Krumboltz, counselor behavior should be designed to arrange situational conditions in ways that foster client acquisition of new and more effective adaptive behaviors.

Bijou (1966) conceives of the counselor as a behavioral engineer "whose function it is to arrange and rearrange the environment in order to bring about desired changes in behavior." Bijou describes four tasks implied by a behavioral science approach to counseling: (1) modifying the problem behavior directly, (2) isolating and dealing with one problem behavior at a time, (3) recording problem behavior in terms of observations of the frequency of occurrence, and (4) changing behavior in the desired direction in small progressive steps.

Summary

Behavioral definitions of counseling emphasize the application of learning theory and experimental psychology to human adjustment and effectiveness. The focus is on the counselor as a facilitator in the learning process. The counselor is concerned with the relationship between environmental changes that foster changes in behavioral responses. Counselors operating from the behavioral point of view use euphemisms such as "social reinforcement machine", "behavioral engineer", and "architect of change" to describe their function. Counseling is seen as an attempt to facilitate the learning process through the explication of the relationship between the client's behavioral responses and his environment. This explication is seen to aid the development process and broaden the range of problem solving and coping responses in the client's repertoire.

A DEVELOPMENTAL BASELINE FOR COUNSELING THEORY

Since counseling emphasizes human effectiveness, it is useful to consider criteria for judging effectiveness within the framework of maturation. It is a widely accepted point of view that human growth occurs both systematically and sequentially. One stage of maturity, in laying the ground work for a later stage, must be achieved before the individual can grow in the manner expected of him as a function of his individual characteristics and social environment. Usually, physiological development must precede the appearance of more advanced psychological behavior. The old axiom, "the child must walk before he can run", is correct in view of knowledge about the development of behavior. In many infrahuman species, specific behavior sequences occur, largely reflecting the organisms' physiological development. In humans, physiological status is no less important to growth and maturity, but its importance is moderated by another set of events. Social-cultural forces enter into the stream of events which influence the developmental sequence seen in human beings. Some of these social-cultural events are instrumental in eliciting behaviors from the individual for which he already possesses response capability as a function of his physiological growth.

The behaviors which are an outcome of these socially determined and physiologically based behaviors are often called developmental tasks because they represent behaviors that most individuals of a given level of maturity can perform, and which are required or elicited by the society in which he lives. To the degree that an individual can successfully perform these tasks, he is, in part, deemed to be maturing satisfactorily and may move along to later developmental tasks. Tasks of one sort or another are required of him all throughout life and serve as guidelines for judgments to be made about success within his subculture. The tasks themselves may be fairly pervasive in society, such as gaining independence from family, or they may be highly specific to certain subgroups in a culture, such as the successful completion of a college degree at one of several selected schools.

What is important about the tasks is that to some extent they structure the kinds of problems that people encounter and the decisions that individuals make about these problems. Developmental tasks create the tensions which lead clients to consult counselors. Developmental tasks change as a function of maturation and situational events. Some problems, thus conceived, may really be self-limiting or situation specific. For example, a student encountering difficulty with his academic requirements may find himself experiencing severe emotional distress. Remove him from the academic environment and the distress may disappear entirely, since his inability to perform the academic tasks required of him was the principle antecedent of his emotional problems.

Many other problems may be viewed in a similar way. Problems of acceptance by peers in adolescence, dating behavior and corollary heterosexual conduct in college students, early establishment in marriage, etc., may really be transitory situationally exacerbated problems. This does not make them any the less disruptive, but it does permit a different perspective to be placed upon them, and allows the counselor to consider objectives other than total client personality change. The counselor can exert his efforts to help his client deal with developmental tasks more effectively at points of discontinuity.

Knowledge about developmental tasks provides the counselor with a set of norms and standards against which to compare client behavior. Developmental perspective suggests potentially productive areas of difficulty to explore with a client. Discontinuities in life seem to occur in predictable ways which are associated with developmental tasks. At these change points, events sometimes go awry or clients may need help in reaching decisions about what steps to take next. Just as a physician with an elderly patient will be alert to signs of various degenerative diseases in contrast to the symptoms of childhood diseases the pediatrician looks for, so a counselor working with an adolescent should be sensitive to problems reflecting the developmental tasks of independence from family, career-oriented educational decisions, and the development of heterosexual skills as opposed to the different requirements associated with the retirement, physical change and the greater imminence of death facing the 65 year old.

The sequence of developmental tasks throughout the life span and the patterns of maturation that individuals exhibit have a regularity that has led to the concept of the *developmental stage*. Developmental stages were systematically formulated by Buehler (1933) who distinguished between the stages of growth (birth to age 14), exploration (to age 25), maintenance (to age 65), and decline (to death). So stated, developmental stages remain fairly general, and not as useful to counselors as they might be. Consequently, the stages have since been subdivided in various ways.

Brammer and Shostrom (1960) cite two general stages of psychological growth, a mastery stage occurring from birth to age 35, during which time the individual is unfolding, and a consolidating stage occurring from age 35 on, during which time the individual elaborates upon the earlier growth. Brammer and Shostrom further subdivide the two large stages of development. Early childhood consists of stages descriptively called the dependency, independence, and role-taking stages, during which time the developmental tasks encountered center around the expression of affection, hostility, aggression, dependency, and early learnings about dealing with sexual tensions. In Brammer and Shostrom's view, the stages are of longer duration as the child grows older. A person moves through a conformity stage, a preadolescent-transition stage, and a synthesis stage in which he must deal with mate and career selection as well as become wholesomely independent of his parental home. From about age 22 to the mid-30's he encounters the so-called experimentation stage, further extending his heterosexual and vocational skills and experiences. From age 35 to 50, he consolidates his earlier growth, followed by an involutional or turning in stage until about age 60, whereupon he enters an evaluation stage which terminates life. The Brammer and Shostrom view is heavily laden with Freudian concepts of development, and describes the developmental tasks largely in terms of social roles.

Blocher (1966) proposes a similar sequence of development and includes social roles, but also includes somewhat specific sets of developmental tasks required at particular age levels, as well as coping behaviors. Thus, in his exploration stage (corresponding roughly to Brammer and Shostrom's experimentation stage), the developmental tasks and coping behaviors include such activities as learning intimacy and commitment, learning to commit oneself to goals, and learning sexual behaviors and risk-taking behaviors. These behaviors may be seen in somewhat more concrete terms than those of Brammer and Shostrom, and consequently, may be of more value to the counselor in determining behavior goals for clients and in assessing the client's behavioral adequacy than has been the case. The behaviorally-oriented counselor can describe in operational terms some behaviors that are likely to produce increases in the probability of establishing, for example, intimate relationships.

The developmental nature of behavior highlights one more important concept. That is, organisms must possess the structural apparatus related to the performance of any specific behavior before any method to teach them that behavior will be effective. Proper neurological, muscular, and skeletal development must precede the development of walking; in humans, no amount of development or training methods will be effective in teaching flying (without the aid of a mechanical contrivance).

Awareness of behaviors associated with developmental tasks can be a very substantial aid to the counselor concerned with behavior change. The shy adolescent can be helped by the counselor's emphasis upon the development of very specific social behaviors, for example, taking steps to be in the presence of people, smiling, listening behaviors; the adolescent who is having difficulty in educational decision-making can learn specific exploratory behaviors; the young mother overwhelmed by the demands of child rearing can develop specific coping behaviors. While the behaviors demanded by the stage are likely to be present in the client's repertoire prior to counseling, the counselor can contribute to the client's ability to identify, practice, and bring to bear the behaviors specifically appropriate to the problem situation.

COUNSELING FOR BEHAVIOR CHANGE

The approaches to counseling theory described earlier deal with human behavior distinctively and in a manner internally consistent with one particular theory. Viewed from another perspective, however, it is apparent that counseling theories share many concepts and counselor behaviors (Patterson, 1966). The examination of these shared attributes might be considered to be "horizontal" in nature, in that it ranges across the diverse theoretical formulations about counseling.

The horizontal analysis of the theories brings attentions to bear principally upon two polar theoretical issues. The first is whether the counseling task is to be seen mainly as interventionistic in nature as opposed to facilitative. Some views maintain that counseling should primarily be oriented towards problem solving (e.g. Krumboltz, 1966b). The focus of counseling activities should be upon the development of methods to identify the causes of discomfort, or of poor performance in the client, and ways to eliminate these causes either through learning procedures or situational manipulations. Those who share this attitude are concerned with the role the counselor plays as an agent of change.

Other points of view about counseling maintain that while attention may at times be directed toward problem solving, the highest objective of counseling is the facilitation of normal development and individual creativity. The epitome of this point of view is perhaps that suggested by the writings of Carl Rogers (1942, 1951). Those who follow this approach are reluctant to see themselves as change makers and prefer instead to work to provide an atmosphere conducive to development of client insight. A major point of difference is who, client or counselor, takes the lead in planning for change.

The second main issue highlighted by a horizontal view of counseling theory is the identification of the major variables upon which counseling activities shall be focused. There seem to be two major objectives related to these variables, namely, change in affective state and cognitive change. Clients seek counseling because of their inability to deal with the environment as effectively as desired, and with the hope that the counselor can assist in the development of improved coping techniques. Counseling for behavior change in this sense is part of every counseling viewpoint though some theorists are more explicit and denotative about their behavioral goals than are others.

Theories which emphasize the change in client affective state are primarily concerned with the role that emotional factors play in producing and maintaining the ineffective behaviors of the client. Counselors oriented in such a way are closely attuned to client feelings. Their view is that the client has failed to develop higher level behaviors (or that he has developed behaviors which interfere with effectiveness) because of the disruptive effect of his emotional life. Presumably, were the client freed from the distorting effects of his inappropriate emotional responses, he could attend to the development of constructive and relevant behaviors. Consequently, counselor efforts are spent in helping the client identify those emotional responses that are inappropriate and which lead to the distortion of everyday events.

Cognitively oriented counseling theorists assume that effective client behaviors are lacking because the client has, for one reason or another, found his ineffective behaviors to be moderately satisfying. Such a counselor's goal is to use the client's rational resources to extinguish the moderately effective behaviors and replace them with more effective behaviors. In attempting to do this, he applies a set of interview procedures that generally stem from a reinforcement view of learning, though they could, and occasionally do, include associational learning concepts.

To some extent, all counseling has as its aim the changing of both cognitive and affective responses, but it is clear that the theories vary with respect to their emphasis on these objectives. The point of view that may be called interventionistic generally focuses on those behavior changes which most often may be mediated by alterations in cognitive processes, while the facilitative theories are more frequently concerned with behavior change mediated through changes in affective responses.

These two dimensions of counseling theory exert a profound influence upon the counseling procedures to be used, the atmosphere within which these counseling procedures occur, and the content upon which the counseling focuses. The interventionistic views, oriented as they are toward behavior change accomplished through cognitive processes, emphasize human rationality and learning theory. In counseling from this view, efforts are devoted to the specific identification of the distressing behavior, the situation within which it occurs, its origin, its maintenance, and environmental features which can be enlisted to change the entire behavioral sequence. Logically, then, interviews, beyond establishing a working rapport, should focus upon details, descriptive diagnostic data collection about events concerned with the troubling situations and behavior. Following data collection the counselor introduces procedures designed to allow the client to change the context within which he operates in a manner which disrupts the system in which the undesired behavior occurs, and, as a result, works toward freeing the client to engage in more desirable behaviors than he could formerly engage in. Later interviews are devoted to practice and feedback, and possibly the identification of new problem situations which might be attacked in a similar manner. Affective responses of the client are dealt with by the counselor as necessary, but the counselor copes with those responses mainly in an effort to eliminate their disruptive effect on the learning process or to use them as motivators for the emission of new responses and subsequent practice.

In sharp contrast, the facilitative view, also committed to behavior change, but not in the same way as the interventionistic view, focuses on the client's affective state and emotional responses to his problem situation. From this point of view, cognitive material is viewed in much the same way that affective material is seen by the interventionists. It is seen as interview material to be eliminated unless it can be enlisted in the cause of dealing with the troublesome affective responses more appropriately. Generally, such theorists expect the major contribution of counseling to be in the area of affective change, and not infrequently these theorists avoid the exploration of cognitive avenues toward behavior change.

It is with respect to this last attitude that the interventionistic-behavior-change-through-cognitive-processes counselor seems to have a major advantage over his colleagues. The goals for any series of counseling interviews are developed by the client and counselor in concert. Thus, if affective responses seem to be to be the client behaviors that are causing distress or disruption, the counselor may seek to introduce procedures to modify these responses via facilitative-affective or cognitive-interventionistic means. However, the reverse rarely holds. It would be surprising to find a facilitative-affectively oriented counselor willing to modify ineffective cognitions. The interventionistic-cognitive counselor seems, thus, to possess more flexibility in the techniques with which to bring about behavior change that are logically consistent with his view than does his facilitative-affective counterpart.

Outcomes of cases approached from the two points of view should be somewhat different. The facilitative-affective counselor hopes to leave his client feeling better and thinking differently, expecting that these changes in covert responses will eventually lead the client to behave differently. The counselor assumes that clients who feel better about themselves and their world will behave differently and more effectively than they did before, but the production of overt changes in client behavior is not crucial to the counselor's judgments about case outcome. The interventionistic-cognitive counselor wants his client to behave differently following counseling and expects that his new and presumably more effective behaviors should make him feel better and think differently but, parallel to the facilitative-affective counselor, changes in the feeling state of the client following counseling are not crucial to his assessments of outcome.

SUMMARY

In this chapter, a variety of approaches to counseling have been reviewed. These various theoretical ideas have been conceived of along two continua, one an affective-cognitive dimension, the other a facilitative-interventionistic one.

A comparison of the two points of view, interventionistic-cognitive (IC) and facilitative-affective (FA), reveals several significant points of difference. The IC viewpoint emphasizes problem solving. The counseling activities of the IC counselor focus on the development of methods to identify causes of client ineffectiveness, poor performance or discomfort, and toward the elimination of the undesired behaviors and the introduction of new and more effective behaviors by means of learning principles. In contrast, the FA viewpoint has the higher human objective of facilitating normal development and individual creativity. As a result, its counseling activities encourage the client to look inward and develop, through verbalized introspection, insights into his behavior that can be used to foster growth. The viewpoint of this book follows the IC approach, which is seen as inclusive of the techniques and concepts of the FA view.

REFERENCES

Arbuckle, D. S. *Counseling: philosophy, theory, and practice.* Boston: Allyn and Bacon, 1965.

Bijou, S. W. Implications of behavioral science for counseling and guidance. In Krumboltz, J. D. (Ed.), *Revolution in counseling.* Boston: Houghton Mifflin, 1966.

Blocher, D. H. *Developmental counseling.* New York: Ronald, 1966.

Bordin, E. S. *Psychological counseling* (First Edition). New York: Appleton-Century-Crofts, 1955.

Bordin, E. S. *Psychological counseling* (Revised Edition). New York: Appleton-Century-Crofts, 1968.

Buehler, C. *Der menschliche Lebenslau als psychologiches Problem.* Leipzig: Hirzel, 1933.

Division of Counseling Psychology, Committee on Definitions. Counseling psychology as a specialty. *American Psychologist,* 1956, *11,* 282-285.

Division of Counseling Psychology, Special Committee. The current status of counseling psychology. Washington, D.C., American Psychological Association, 1961.

Dollard, J. and Miller, N. E. *Personality and psychotherapy.* New York: McGraw-Hill, 1950.

Ellis, A. *Reason and emotion in psychotherapy.* New York: Lyle Stuart, 1962.

English, H. B. and English, A. C. *A comprehensive dictionary of psychological and psychiatric terms.* New York: McKay, 1958.

Ford, D. H. and Urban, H. B. *Systems of psychotherapy.* New York: Wiley, 1963.

Frankl, V. E. *Man's search for meaning.* Boston: Beacon, 1962.

Gustad, J. W. The definition of counseling. In Berdie, R. F. (Ed.), *Roles and relationships in counseling.* Minneapolis: University of Minnesota, 1953.

Kaam, A. L. van. Counseling and psychotherapy from the viewpoint of existential psychology. In Arbuckle, D. S. (Ed.), *Counseling and psychotherapy: an overview.* New York: McGraw-Hill, 1967.

Kelly, G. A. *The psychology of personal constructs.* (Two volumes) New York: Norton, 1955.

Krasner, L. The therapist as a social reinforcement machine. In H. Strupp and L. Luborsky (Eds.), *Research in Psychotherapy,* Vol. II, Washington, D.C.: American Psychological Association, 1962.

Krumboltz, J. D. Behavioral goals for counseling. *Journal of Counseling Psychology,* 1966, *13,* 153-159. (a)

Krumboltz, J. D. (Ed.) *Revolution in counseling.* Boston: Houghton Mifflin, 1966. (b)

Oetting, E. R. Developmental definition of counseling psychology. *Journal of Counseling Psychology,* 1967, *14,* 382-385.

Osipow, S. H. *Theories of career development.* New York: Appleton-Century-Crofts, 1968.

Patterson, C. H. *Theories of counseling and psychotherapy.* New York: Harper and Row, 1966.

Patterson, C. H. Psychotherapy in the school. In Arbuckle, D. S. (Ed.), *Counseling and psychotherapy.* New York: McGraw-Hill, 1967.

Pepinsky, H. B. and Pepinsky, P. N. *Counseling: theory and practice.* New York: Ronald, 1954.

Perez, J. F. *Counseling: theory and practice.* Reading, Massachusetts: Addison-Wesley, 1965.

Phillips, E. L. and Wiener, D. N. *Short-term psychotherapy and structured behavior change.* New York: McGraw-Hill, 1966.

Rogers, C. R. *Counseling and psychotherapy.* Boston: Houghton Mifflin, 1942.

Rogers, C. R. *Client-centered therapy.* Boston: Houghton Mifflin, 1951.

Rotter, J. B. *Social learning and clinical psychology.* Englewood Cliffs, New Jersey: Prentice-Hall, 1954.

Shostrom, E. L. and Brammer, L. M. *The dynamics of the counseling process.* New York: McGraw-Hill, 1952.

Skinner, B. F. *Science and human behavior.* New York: Macmillan, 1953.

Stefflre, B. (Ed.), *Theories of counseling.* New York: McGraw-Hill, 1965.

Tyler, L. *The work of the counselor.* New York: Appleton-Century-Crofts, 1961.

Ullmann, L. P. and Krasner, L. Introduction. In Ullmann, L. P. and Krasner, L. (Eds.), *Case studies in behavior modification.* New York: Holt, Rinehart, and Winston, 1965.

Watson, R. I. The experimental tradition and clinical psychology. In Bachrach, A. J. (Ed.), *Experimental foundations of clinical psychology.* New York: Basic Books, 1962.

Wiener, N. *Cybernetics.* New York: Wiley, 1948.

Williamson, E. G. *Counseling adolescents.* New York: McGraw-Hill, 1950.

Wolberg, L. R. *The technique of psychotherapy.* New York: Grune and Stratton, 1954.

Wolpe, J. *Psychotherapy by reciprocal inhibition.* Stanford: Stanford University Press, 1958.

Wrenn, C. G. *Student personnel work in college.* New York: Ronald, 1951.

Chapter 2

Assessment

THE TRADITIONAL VIEW

The concept of diagnosis in counseling is based on the model developed by medicine. In medical practice, patients are scrutinized for symptoms which would suggest the presence of some central disease process or tissue deterioration which might be reversed or terminated through pharmaceutical or surgical intervention. If the physician cannot identify the nature of the disease process, or if medical science is not acquainted with the antecedents of the disorder, or if there is no known procedure which effectively halts or reverses the disease process, then efforts are expended largely toward symptom remission or control, with the objective of making the patient as comfortable as possible despite the ailment. A major concern growing out of the medical model of diagnosis is the development of a suitable taxonomy classifying diseases in order to facilitate the identification of specific treatments that are likely to be differentially effective in dealing with different disorders.

In counseling, the concept of diagnosis and its use has been substantially changed from that in medicine, although efforts at developing useful taxonomies in counseling diagnosis exist. The major goals of diagnosis in counseling have not been related to the development of a differential-diagnosis differential-treatment effort. Instead, diagnosis has concerned itself with screening groups of individuals with regard to their potential for adjustment under various circumstances, determing "prognosis" for changing various disruptive behavior patterns, identifying possible major treatment approaches (interview, collaboration with medical resources, situational changes, family involvement, institutionalization, etc.), and identifying "sensitive" content areas about which to focus the counseling interviews.

Counselors also use the notion of diagnosis in a special way when they perform an appraisal to aid an individual in reaching an educational or vocational decision. As examples, there are Williamson's (1950) diagnostic plan: identifying the problem, its causes, and its prognosis, which in reality instructs us about how to proceed in performing the diagnostic task; Pepinsky's (1948) plan of sorting problems into areas such as dependency, lack of information, self-conflict, lack of assurance and lack of skill; and Bordin's (1946) scheme which shares the dependency, lack of information, and self-conflict categories but substitutes choice anxiety and "no problem" for lack of assurance and lack of skill. The proposals of Pepinsky and Bordin go part of the way toward differential diagnosis and differential treatment in their identification of a problem area, but they do not lead to specific treatments. Treatments distinctively related to the problems are not evident because the categories are neither explicit nor mutually exclusive; thus, the treatments for problems in different categories overlap extensively.

Generally, the traditional diagnostic task in counseling has been approached loosely, partly because some counselors can see no utility to the task since it has not led to specific treatment procedures in the way medical diagnosis ideally does. Other counselors have questioned the distinction between diagnosis and treatment, and still others object to the judgmental aspect of diagnosis claiming that it interferes with the client-counselor relationship. Indeed, the client-centered counselor objects to diagnosis on all three counts. The client-centered view of counseling assures a single etiology of client difficulty and, consequently, a single treatment, so that formal diagnosis is neither logical nor necessary.

DIAGNOSIS AND INTERVENTIONIST-COGNITIVE COUNSELING

It is useful to consider diagnosis in the context of the interventionistic-cognitive viewpoint described in Chapter 1. The IC approach to counseling is aimed toward problem solving, decision making, and overt behavior change. In other words, it emphasizes an active seeking of methods to deal effectively with *events* as well as *thoughts*. The counselor, acting consistently with this goal, plays an active role in counseling, using himself as an extension, in a way, of the client, but not using the client as an extension of himself. When he asks the client questions, he is really helping the client identify questions to ask himself, questions that may lead to a productive accumulation of data about the client, his world, and how he interacts with it. Diagnosis helps the counselor make the decisions that he must make to counsel effectively. Questions such as: is another interview necessary; need the client be referred; is medical intervention necessary or appropriate; do we need a family consultation and is it likely to be useful; what are priorities of client concern; what must be dealt with first; does the client need counseling; if so, when, what kind, and how often does he need to be seen; can my skills help rather than hurt him (personal adjustment counseling might be in order but that might lead to overlooking achievement problems which might be exacerbated); does he need treatment in another setting; can he live with his problem more easily than change his behavior; will occasional ventilation be all he needs; is a minor situational manipulation likely to be useful; does he need a probing analytic approach; and what objectives are reasonable? The previous list is an example of the many questions that must be answered in relatively short order by the counselor. Obviously, both data and their evaluation are necessary.

In the light of the importance of the decisions that counselors must make about their clients and the appropriate counseling activities, concern over issues such as whether or not diagnostic activity influences client behavior, whether or not it detracts from client-counselor relationship, or whether it can be clearly separated from treatment, seems somewhat irrelevant. There is no evidence that negative results accrue from diagnosis. The strongest objections to diagnosis on theoretical grounds stem from the client-centered and existential counselors who are fearful of imposing their views on clients but who ignore the possibility that a counselor's views may be imposed as much by what he fails to do as by what he does.

MODERN VIEWS OF DIAGNOSIS

The traditional concept of diagnosis has gradually been undergoing revision. When counseling first became formalized, attention was given to the task of diagnosis, but efforts declined over the years. The decline was partly the result of the influence of the client-centered view, which sees diagnosis as inimical to client growth, and partly because differential techniques for use with clients with different diagnoses were slow to be developed. Nevertheless, the concept has evolved as some counselors continued to explore ways in which their effectiveness in dealing with certain kinds of client problems might be improved. The newer viewpoints are not based on the disease model of medical diagnosis which assumes a central core of disorder whose effects radiate outward. According to the disease model the disorder causes overt symptoms from which inferences may be made concerning the nature of the underlying disorder. Instead, the new approaches view behavior disruptions primarily as problems in human learning and see diagnosis as a task which consists of eliciting data from the client on whose basis inferences about the development of the problematic behavior may be generated. Further, it is assumed that the identification of original learning conditions will be helpful in developing procedures that may be introduced to remedy ineffective behaviors. These views are well represented by Ford and Urban (1963) and by Krumboltz (1965; 1966 a; b; c). The approach is not taxonomically oriented but inference oriented, and more specific with respect to the particular behaviors of interest to the counselor than were the earlier efforts at diagnosis for counseling. As a consequence, inferential diagnosis possesses a greater potential for the development of differential techniques to be used in counseling than disease model diagnosis. A related benefit of this advantage is the greater potential for generating useful counseling outcome studies that inferential approaches possess.

The goals of the newer view are the same as those of the earlier ones. The difference is that the medically based diagnostic schemes assume that where a common etiology exists, a generally common symptomatology and treatment for disorders exist. The more recently developed views explicitly aim to identify antecedents to the problem behavior and, perhaps even more significantly, are concerned with specifying those events which cause the problem behavior to be maintained, as distinguished from naming those instrumental in its genesis. The emphasis on the identification of antecedents leads to a behavioral focus. Krumboltz (1966) talks about setting specific and individual behavior goals for clients. For the shy client, the goal might be increasing the frequency of his interaction with others, the reduction of overt manifestations of discomfort in interactions with groups of three or more individuals, and a diminution of subjective reports of stress related to social interaction. For the lonely client, behaviors representing attempts to initiate interactions with others are to be specified and considered appropriate goals. Diagnosis in this sense, then, is the homing in upon specific problem behaviors, identifying their environmental and personal antecedents, and developing procedures to extinguish old behaviors (if necessary) and acquire new ones.

COUNSELOR BEHAVIOR

The counselor operating from the point of view of the interventionistic-cognitive theory typically engages in a successive process in his casework. First comes a situational assessment, followed by the identification of relevant antecedents, the identification of ways of treating the client within the interview or interview-like setting, and finally, the development of bridges connecting changes generated by means of the interview procedures to significant behaviors and events occurring outside of the interview.

To accomplish these objectives the effective counselor engages in two streams of behavior. On a conceptual level, he develops hypotheses and makes inferences on the basis of his observations of the client's behavior. Questions are framed about client bahavior and the context within which it occurs in order to identify more clearly the antecedents and maintainers of the response. Simultaneously, the counselor's overt responses communicate interest, sensitivity, and "authenticity" to the client, without which the data necessary to make the aforesaid judgments might not be forthcoming from the client and without which the counselor will have difficulty in acquiring the reinforcing value that it is necessary for him to have to become an effective agent of change. The counselor must behave in a manner which will effectively produce a particular climate.

In other words, the counselor must distinguish between his efforts to understand the basis of the client's behavior and what is troublesome about it on the one hand, and his efforts to identify the behavior he must engage in to help bring about appropriate changes in the client. The former is theory, the latter technique; both are important. The combination of these two presents the counselor with a formidable task (Goldman, 1967).

The counseling task can basically be divided into four kinds of events. First, it is necessary to *identify* the behaviors that shall be of primary concern in counseling. Since clients behave 24 hours per day, no counselor can attend to all aspects of client behavior. As a consequence, one of the first efforts of the counselor is to delineate those behaviors, in as concrete terms as possible, more likely to be intimately connected with client counseling objectives, i.e., the problematic behaviours. Secondly, he must *assess* the behaviors so identified; in other words, it is necessary to observe the behavior in a way which communicates how much or how often the client engages in those behaviors deemed to be relevant to the counseling objectives. Thirdly, the counselor must *evaluate* the behaviors from the point of view of strategies for counseling. Is the particular behavior (and there may be many to be evaluated for any given client) to be maintained, can it be enlisted to facilitate change, need it be extinguished, suppressed, or inhibited temporarily, what does it tell us about the troublesome behavior, and so on. These three stages are all really part of the diagnostic activity; the fourth stage, *change*, is what should happen following diagnosis, and includes the systematic efforts of the counselor on the basis of the previous diagnostic work to modify client behaviour, to teach the client how to maintain those changes, and to observe the persistence of the new behaviors on later occasions.

DIAGNOSTIC METHODS

The role of antecedents. The task of identifying the behaviors of concern in counseling may be most productively approached by means of searching for specific behaviors and events in the client's history which seem closely connected with the events about which the client is complaining. The counselor will usually find it profitable to ask himself the question: what stream of behavioral events might have originated the current disruptive or ineffective behaviors? For example, if the client complains of an inability to make friends (deferring for the moment the counselor's efforts to have the client operationally describe what that means), the counselor would strive to identify those events in the client's immediate past through which response styles might have been unwittingly acquired which interfere with making friends. For example, one individual might have learned to inhibit socially related behaviors as a result of familial demands to excel academically. Another person might have acquired social behaviors appropriate to the subculture he then lived in but which interfere with acceptance in his new circle. A third individual may be engaging in covert verbal responses which reflect his fear that his social overtures may be rejected, and these may inhibit those very behaviors which might lead to his social acceptance (and the extinction of the anticipatory fear responses).

The antecedents of concern, then, for the first client would be inferred from his description of his family background, his lack of social activity previously, the reasons for it, and the resulting lack of social facility. The counseling task for such a client would probably involve a relatively simple acquisition task. Important antecedents for the second client, whose social behaviors were inappropriate to the new situation, lie in his descriptions of his earlier social activities and successes, thus leading to the inference that he once possessed socially effective responses which are now ineffective. Counseling with this client would involve extinguishing one set of overt behaviors and reinforcing the acquisition of a new set to replace them. For the third client, the critical antecedent events are the subjective fear responses. With this client it might be necessary to discover the antecedents of the subjective responses. In any event, the counseling task with this individual would be the extinction of the fear responses, the acquisition of socially seeking responses, and the acquisition of socially related behaviors. Thus, it can be seen, antecedent conditions play a large role in disclosing the private events for the client that the overt complaints may represent, but they do so in a way which lends themselves to operationism and client-counselor manipulation.

The role of the situation. It should be clear from the discussion of antecedents, that knowledge of situational factors is of considerable importance to the counselor. Of primary significance is the impact situational manipulations of client living conditions may have in helping the client effect change. Also of importance is counselor awareness of situational factors that may hasten the identification of relevant antecedents. These concerns lead to an analysis of the circumstances and conditions under which the ineffective behavior patterns originated.

Osipow and Grooms (1970) have illustrated a number of ways that situational manipulation may be used productively in counseling. In one kind of situation, an individual may be led to expose himself systematically to two kinds of situations which will provide him with feedback which may prove useful to him in making a decision and evaluating it with confidence. For example, using this approach with a student undecided about academic alternatives, a counselor would strive to have the student build academic schedules, either sequentially or concurrently, that can provide a sample of the crucial aspects of two or more alternatives. Feedback from such a plan would include differences in performance potential and subjective feelings of satisfaction associated with the different academic programs.

Another use of situational analysis is to help the client identify those transient aspects of his life which may be contributing to an acute and disruptive emotional episode. When disruption occurs in response to temporary circumstances an individual might find it simpler to avoid the disruptive situation than to try to change his subjective emotional responses to it. Even where the situation cannot or should not be manipulated extensively, knowledge of the specific situational context of a client's life may be helpful in devising ways to bring about periods of temporary relief during which time more durable efforts to bring about behavior changes may be initiated.

Behavioral origination and maintenance. The natural development of a response sequence is likely to be widely separated in time from the events in the individual's environment which contribute to its continuation. In dealing with highly complex learned behavior sequences, counselors, may profitably work toward introducing a distinction between the originators and the maintainers of behaviors. Allport's (1937) concept of the functional autonomy of motives applied to the behavioral realm is a good example of this distinction. Traditionally, much of the counselor's or psychotherapist's effort has been devoted to accumulating historical data about the client aimed at generating information about the events and circumstances under which the behavior of concern originated. Presumably, following this accumulation, the counselor will work toward helping the client distinguish between the rational and irrational aspects of the original learning. The counselor will further help the client distinguish between those aspects of the original situation which may still be applicable and those which are not, thus leading the client to a greater sophistication in discriminating between the differential effects of various stimulus events. As a consequence he should be able to exert a greater control over the effectiveness of his behavior with respect to stimuli, both interpersonal and experiential. Unfortunately, it is rarely, if ever possible, to accumulate enough accurate historical data about the original learning conditions from which to proceed logically to accomplish the desired discriminations. Furthermore, the procedure is extremely time consuming and often lacks face validity for the client, sometimes contributing to his failure to continue with counseling even though both he and the counselor recognize his need to change behavior.

The historical approach also fails to take into sufficient consideration the degree to which responses, once acquired, are subject to subsequent modification and shaping by means of new and partially relevantre inforcements. For example, some maladaptive interpersonal response sequences may be learned during childhood years under authoritarian parents. Later authority figures may behave less irrationally and punitively, and thus, inadvertently, help the client to extinguish a tendency to overgeneralize from his earlier experience. In a negative fashion it is possible for an anxiety reaction toward school to develop in a child out of fear that a dog will attack him on the way to and from school, and for the anxiety reaction to interfere with adjustment in school leading to academic failure. Years later, the anxiety, now maintained because of academically related fears, will persist despite the disappearance of the dog or fear of dogs. To a therapist who identifies the origination of the school anxiety without discovering its newer implications, the failure of the anxiety to dissipate after the situational element changed may be puzzling. Furthermore, a deconditioning therapy aimed at reducing the fear reaction produced by dogs may be effective in reducing that source of anxiety, but will not be likely to generalize and thus fail to reduce the newer antecedents of anxiety.

In some cases, then, the historical approach may even be misleading, since it might not take the counselor far enough along in the stream of events in the client's life to locate current sources of difficulty. Should such a client explain his fears regarding school in terms of his current anxiety about the adequacy of his performance, some counselors would not be satisfied, but would persist in pressing backward historically until some such set of incidents like the dog fear were discovered.

Setting behavioral goals for counseling. From the point of view of the interventionistic-cognitive approach a major part of the diagnostic task is the identification of specific behavioral goals to be achieved by the client, in the manner suggested by Krumboltz (1966b, 1966c). On the basis of observations of the client behavior and on the basis of client self-report, the counselor should be able to determine a number of the client's specific behavioral patterns that recur and that cause him difficulty. As part of the assessment phase of the interview series, the counselor should be able to describe, to both his and the client's satisfaction, ways that the client would behave were he responding effectively and appropriately. Ideally, more change is to be hoped for than merely getting the client to talk differently about himself during the interviews. The most desirable behaviors to be developed are actions which would prove to be instrumental in changing either the client's interpersonal effectiveness, his efficiency in his work, his subjective evaluations of his overall competence, or combinations of the three. Tasks can be operationally determined for all three categories, much as Krumboltz (1966a) has suggested. Lists of these tasks also serve well as a criterion against which to evaluate counseling effectiveness later.

The first type of concern, interpersonal effectiveness, is usually presented as a vague complaint by the client. He may describe himself as lonely, unhappy, bored, restless, as unable to communicate with others, unable to make friends, etc. Behaviors reflecting effectiveness in reducing these *complaints* might be the development of socializing responses, such as increasing the frequency of greeting others, smiling, joining clubs and attending meetings, volunteering for positions involving responsibility and action in those clubs, behaviors of seeking the company of others, acquiring knowledge and skills which provide content about which to talk to others and mutual interests, etc. The list can and should reflect behaviors specifically needed by the client.

Complaints concerning effectiveness in work, too, may initially be vague and unspecified, and the counselor should try to elicit as high a degree of concreteness from the client as he reasonably can. A client complains of inability to concentrate on his studies, or he may ask to take an aptitude test, or he may complain of his lack of motivation concerning his academic work; the employee feels vaguely that he is not advancing satisfactorily, or that the work is boring and fails to offer variety. Once again, the counselor's task is to elicit information concerning concrete client behaviors relevant to these complaints. In doing so, he might find that changes in a client's studying routine might enable him to exert more control over his attending responses. Thus, learning how to externalize some aspects of studying (note taking, outlining) that require active participation rather than passive involvement (such as underlining) might maintain the student's activity level at a higher point and reduce wanderings in concentration because of the student's ability to specify behaviorally the tasks involved in studying. Also, for the same reasons, the student will be able to identify earlier than before occasions when his attention begins to wander. The dissatisfied employee should determine specific events that would imply advancement to him, and search for specific behaviors he can engage in to facilitate that advancement. What can he do that will demonstrate his usefulness to his employer?

The third type of situation, dealing effectively with subjective evaluations the client makes of himself, is more difficult than the two previous problems. Even here, however, the counselor can take the approach of eliciting from the client statements which represent the specific aspects of these self-derogatory subjective judgments. Once the client has satisfactorily explicated some of the verbal components of these judgments, they may be translated into behavioral events which can then be modified. Another possibility is client recognition of the degree to which his subjective evaluations do not match the overt behaviors which should reflect them, and thus he may learn to modify his subjective judgments in the presence of more realistic and less private feedback about his personal value. In this way his judgments will not be as susceptible to internal distortion.

Diagnostic subroles for counselors. Sullivan's (1954) terms for the diagnostic activities of the therapist are usefully modified for the counselor. For present purposes, the assessment phase of the counseling case may be considered to occur in three segments. The first of these, in Sullivan's terms, may be called the *inception*. During this phase, which occurs at the initiation of client-counselor contact, the counselor's objective is the development of rapport in order to acquire the necessary information upon which to base a counseling plan as well as the clear establishment of the client's motives for counseling. Behaviorally, the counselor strives to elicit client verbalization so that it pours forth smoothly and with cogency to the client concern. With some clients, this opening phase may be brief; with others, it may take more than two or three interviews. In this subrole the counselor is fundamentally reflective and uses those techniques which reinforce client talk.

Once the client has presented what is in his view a comprehensive account of his concern, the counselor shifts into the second diagnostic subrole, called, again in Sullivan's terms, the *reconnaissance*. Here the counselor becomes somewhat more active than before, leading the client to talk briefly about aspects of his life which may not apparently be directly related to his presented concerns. Thus, the client who presents a problem concerning his inability to concentrate on his studies would be led, during reconnaissance, to discuss aspects of his life which would give the counselor information about his adequacy in other areas of his life, such as social life, career decisions, family relationships, health, and so on. In that way the counselor can begin to get some idea about what and how the client's life in general is related to the opening complaint. The counselor might, for example, learn that the study problem is the result of inefficiency brought on by the client's preoccupation with his lack of interpersonal effectiveness. If this were to be the case the ensuing approach to the problem would be considerably different than if the problem were what it originally seemed to be, i.e., a lack of study procedures effective in reducing the frequency of irrelevant thought patterns during studying.

The third diagnostic subrole may be called the *detailed inquiry*. During this portion of casework the counselor becomes even more active and searches for details concerning the specific conditions under which the troublesome behavior occurs. The object, of course, is to come to some conclusion about what the behavior represents. The counselor would want to know the conditions under which the behavior occurs, its intensity, its frequency, its duration, its pervasiveness and generality, what other behaviors are involved, how disruptive the undesired behavior is to the client's life, its onset, and how it has changed (if it has) since the client first became aware of the problem. In this way the counselor can begin to isolate the behaviors that the client engages in which seem to be related to the troublesome behavior. Tests and inventories might be used in conjunction with this phase of diagnosis. (This role will be discussed in the next chapter.) For the client who finds it difficult to concentrate on his studies, the counselor would want to know, among other things, what behaviors the client sees as involved in concentrating, when the client first noticed difficulty in concentrating, how specific it is to course content, whether he experiences such difficulty even in thinking about affairs not connected with studying, how important it is to him to study, his affective reaction to school work, how often it happens, how long it lasts and how strongly distracted he becomes.

Often the client does not have access to the information the counselor needs since the client has never observed his behavior systematically. The counselor may have to teach him how and what to observe and ask him to do so between interviews. As an alternative, the counselor can strive to recreate the original events vicariously in the interview by having the client review the last concrete episode of difficulty in studying and discussing the detailed issues just described. The basic characteristic of the detailed inquiry phase is its emphasis on concrete events and behaviors.

Sequences and syndromes. The detailed inquiry phase leads directly to the counselor's attempt to specify the behavior sequences of the client that are associated with the behavior of concern. By discussing numerous examples of the troublesome behavior in great detail, the counselor becomes increasingly able to identify the chains of client behaviors, both overt and subjective, and their environmental contexts, which are involved in the creation and maintenance of the disruptive sequence. This identification provides the counselor with ways to explore intervention. (The intervention strategies are discussed in Chapter IV.) The more disruptive behavior sequences the counselor observes in the client, the more pervasive the complaint. Observation of a number of these leads to the concept of behavior syndromes, which are behavior sequences that seem to be highly correlated with one another. For example, one might observe several behavior sequences in a client which lead to a response the client describes as "feeling depressed." This abstraction, feeling depressed, suggests other, consequent, behavior sequences that the client has not mentioned, such as isolative behavior, lethargic behavior, and so on, as well as behavior sequences which are usually associated with events leading up to "feeling depressed." The utility of knowledge of these syndromes, that is, what behaviors seem to go together, is that this provides a short cut to inquiring into client behaviors. In addition, inquiries about them lead to client confidence in the counselor because they indicate implicitly to the client that his counselor is experienced, "understands him", and has encountered problems similar to his before and is neither bewildered nor frightened by him.

Thus, the counselor, drawing upon his experience, recognizes behavioral syndromes. On the basis of the particular syndromes he observes the counselor can predict the probability of the presence of other behaviors associated with a given behavior sequence. In other words, if behaviors A, B, C, E, and F are present, what is the likelihood that D is also occurring?

The absence of such behaviors, or information about their range and intensity, can lead the counselor to make judgments about potentially appropriate avenues to bring about behavior change. The detailed analysis of these sequences is discussed in Chapter 3, while the implications of such analysis for the development of counseling strategies is discussed in Chapter 4.

SUMMARY

This section has compared the traditional, medically based model of diagnosis in counseling with the behavioral approach. One major difference between the two lies in the locus of difficulty and their different implications for counseling. The medical model tends to ignore the treatment of symptoms in its devotion to the resolution of the basic causes of the difficulty, while the behavioral model deals with the symptoms themselves as disruptive learned phenomena. Diagnosis from a behavioral point of view studies behavioral antecedents, situational contributions, distinctions between behavioral originators and behavioral maintainers, and works toward the specification of behavioral objectives for casework.

REFERENCES

Allport, G. W. *Personality*. New York: Holt, 1937.

Bordin, E. S. Diagnosis in counseling and psychotherapy. *Educational and Psychological Measurement*, 1946, *6*, 169-184.

Ford, D. H. and Urban, H. B. *Systems of psychotherapy*. New York: Wiley, 1963.

Goldman, L. Information and counseling: a dilemma. *Personnel and Guidance Journal*, 1967, *46*, 42–46.

Krumboltz, J. D. Behavioral counseling: rationale and research. *Personnel and Guidance Journal*, 1965, *44*, 383-387.

Krumboltz, J. D. Behavioral goals for counseling. *Journal of Counseling Psychology*, 1966, *13*, 153-159. (a)

Krumboltz, J. D. (Ed.), *Revolution in counseling*. Boston: Houghton Mifflin, 1966. (b)

Krumboltz, J. D. Promoting adaptive behavior: new answers to familiar questions. In Krumboltz, J. D. (Ed.), *Revolution in counseling*. Boston: Houghton Mifflin, 1966. (c)

Osipow, S. H. and Grooms, R. R. Behavior modification through situational manipulation. In Osipow, S. H. and Walsh, W. B. (Eds.), *Behavior change in counseling: readings and cases*. New York: Appleton-Century-Crofts, 1970.

Pepinsky, H. B. The selection and use of diagnostic categories in clinical counseling. *Applied Psychology Monographs*, No. 15, 1948.

Sullivan, H. S. *The psychiatric interview*. New York: Norton, 1954.

Williamson, E. G. *Counseling adolescents*. New York: McGraw-Hill, 1950.

Chapter 3

Behavioral Analysis

The focus of the behavioral approach is on overt behavior. Consistent with this orientation is the thought that advances in counseling effectiveness may be related to the behavioral assessment of clients. Behavioral data can be collected that contribute to the development of new behaviors and, thus, aid the counseling process. Assessment provides the information upon which the counseling program is constructed. Therefore, the purpose of this chapter is to develop a taxonomy for behavioral data and to consider methods of collecting and organizing behavioral data so that it can be analyzed adequately.

According to Krasner and Ullmann (1965) assessment begins with identifying disadvantageous behavior, identifying reinforcers that maintain existing behavior, positing new behaviors that can replace the disadvantageous behavior, and identifying potential reinforcers that can be manipulated in order to increase or maintain socially appropriate behavior. Therefore, assessment is based on current behavior in the total environment and specifically focuses on the collection of information about the client's instrumental and mediational responses that are cognitive and affective in nature.

FERSTER'S TOPOGRAPHIC AND FUNCTIONAL ANALYSIS

On the topic of assessment Ferster (1965) presents a frame of reference that is of value. He argues that environmental stimuli determine and maintain inappropriate or disruptive behavior. Consequently, the individual's disruptive behavior is the result of the interaction between his social environment and his history of reinforcement. To Ferster, the society in which an individual lives determines both the content of his behavior and the persons who shape it. In other words, the inappropriate behavior may be defined in terms of the behavior that important people in the individual's environment (his social reinforcers) wish to increase, decrease, or change.

In order to classify behavior Ferster (1965) suggests that both static (topographic analysis) and dynamic (functional analysis) factors be taken into account. Topographic analysis attempts to describe what has occurred, that is, the behavioral performance. Functional analysis involves collecting data about antecedent conditions and the relation of the behavior to the environment. Functional analysis is, thus, an attempt to understand the meaning of the behavior in an environment, while topographic analysis is simply descriptive. For example, whether a college student who is quiet and withdrawn after the completion of final examinations is dejected or merely thinking about other things is not easily determined by just observing his behavior (topographic analysis). The relation of his behavior to conditions in the past or present environment is significant (functional analysis). The student could be withdrawn because of his overall poor performance on exams. The student could be withdrawn because he again failed to pass German. The student could be withdrawn because he is thinking about how he will spend the summer months. The student could be withdrawn because he is thinking about the coming autumn and graduate school. All of these behaviors are quite similar to each other topographically, but functionally they are extremely diverse.

Ferster (1965) believes that the environment specifies the responses potentially available to an individual. The individual's environment may be conceived to possess an infinite number of response keys which may be reinforced or punished in connection with an aversive stimulus if the person's response repertoire possesses the required behaviors. Therefore, the functional analysis of behavior might include an assessment of the behavioral or response potential of the environment. As a result, it becomes possible to compare the individual's response repertoire to the behavioral potential required by the environment for personal effectiveness. The comparison would serve to identify responses missing from an individual's repertoire that the environment is potentially capable of supporting. The acquisition of the missing responses may aid in the reduction of problematic behaviors.

In describing an individual's response repertoire, Ferster suggests two dimensions that serve to maintain behaviors, positive reinforcers and aversive stimuli. A response which produces desired environmental change leads to the increased probability of the emission of that behavior in the future (positive reinforcement). However, a response may occur in order to postpone the effect of or to escape from an aversive situation or stimulus (negative reinforcement). Such a response has a reinforcing effect since it serves to reduce the individual's anxiety response on a short-term basis under unpleasant stimulus conditions. To Ferster, a stimulus is aversive because of its relationship with loss of positive reinforcement. Therefore, a description of an individual's response repertoire which could aid the counseling process would involve the identification of positive reinforcers which control the individual's behaviors, aversive stimuli controlling his behavior, and the relation of the aversive stimuli to the positively reinforced repertoire.

However, the functional analysis of the repertoire cannot easily be made from observations of a limited sample of the behavior. According to Ferster (1965) the analysis must consider the frequency of the behavior in relation to its schedule of reinforcement. Thus, similar repertoires may be caused by different relations to the controlling environment. Also, apparently similar performances may be maintained under quite different conditions.

Another class of behaviors (self-control behavior) permits the individual to alter his behavior to allow more effective response to the environment. Self-control behaviors, according to Ferster (1965), are those responses that alter the relation between the individual's behavior and his controlling environment. For example, the ability to avoid ruminating over depressing events, or to inhibit engaging in an undesired activity such as smoking are instances of control behaviors in which individuals vary. Thus, it is important that a portion of the assessment task should involve the identification of critical variables controlling the individual's behavior. As a result of such identification the counseling process could help the individual acquire discriminating, controlling behaviors which in turn lead to greater control over the individual's exposure to resulting stimuli. Once the individual has acquired specific controlling behaviors he is in a position to bring his behavior under the control of one aspect of the environment in preference to another.

Summary. Ferster (1965) suggests that inappropriate behaviors may be defined in terms of the behavior that significant others in the individual's environment wish to increase, decrease, or change. In classifying behavior, both static (topographic analysis) and dynamic (functional analysis) factors are taken into consideration. The topographic analysis focuses on the behavioral performance. The functional analysis accumulates data on antecedent conditions, the relation of the behavior to the environment, and the meaning of the behavior. In the functional analysis an attempt is made to compare the individual's response repertoire to the behavioral potential of the environment. The comparison serves to identify responses missing from a repertoire; responses that the environment is capable of supporting. In describing a response repertoire the focus is on two dimensions, positive reinforcers and aversive stimuli. Therefore, an attempt to describe a response repertoire would involve the identification of positive reinforcers, aversive stimuli, and the relation of aversive stimuli to the positively reinforced repertoire. However, one must remember that similar repertoires may be the product of different relations to the controlling environment. In essence, Ferster (1965) seems to be saying that a vital portion of the assessment involves the identification of initial variables which control the individual's behavior.

BIJOU'S OBSERVATIONAL TECHNIQUES

The assessment procedure suggested by Bijou (1965) begins by making a count of the frequency of occurrence of an inappropriate behavior in order to determine its baseline frquency. This includes an objective account of antecedent and consequent stimulus events that are potentially related to the occurrence of such responses. The frequency count is carried out before intervention of any kind has occurred. Next, the intervention procedure or the treatment program designed to effect behavior change is introduced. Then, continuous follow-up procedure is implemented to determine if the intervention does in fact change frequency of occurrence of the behavior when compared with the baseline performance.

Bijou, thus, suggests a set of measures that will show changes in the specific behavior under study in counseling, and which therefore permits a continuous assessment of the behavioral impact of counseling. If the records showed that the treatment program was effective (i.e. reduced the frequency of occurrence of undesirable behavior), the counseling program would be continued; if the records showed that the program was ineffective, the program would be modified. The records could accumulate behavioral data, the program attempted and the outcomes at any time during counseling. In addition, the records would contribute to the development of theory and technique that may be used in both service and research. Last, Bijou (1965) believes that such objective measures would be of value in writing reports summarizing case work.

Consistent with the focus on specific behavior is Bijou's procedure of diagnosing in terms of client performance. He suggests a shift in the diagnostic procedure from an analysis of psychological traits to an analysis of psychological functions. An analysis of psychological functions involves collecting behavioral data regarding both what an individual is capable of doing and the identification of the specific conditions most favorable to the desired behavior. The emphasis is on collecting behavioral data that will serve to advance a specific aspect of the counseling process.

Summary. Bijou (1965) suggests identifying and observing the frequency of inappropriate behavior in order to obtain a baseline before intervention of any kind is carried out. He also sees a need for a set of measures that will show changes in the specific behavior under study in counseling, and permit continuous assessment of the counseling. Like Ferster (1965), Bijou (1965) and Peterson (1968) propose a shift in the diagnostic procedure from the current analysis of psychological traits to an analysis of psychological functions.

DIMENSIONS OF BEHAVIOR ANALYSIS

Wolpe and Lazarus (1966) see the need to gather data identifying the stimulus antecedents of responses about which the client complains. The behavioral data serve to inform the therapist about the response pattern exhibited by the client in various situations. Such data aid the therapeutic process by indicating the important situational elements related to the the client's concerns. These data may come from a number of sources—a history of the origin of the client's responses, a review of his personal development, questionnaire data, and the exploration of special attention areas.

The initial step in the data collection process involves a chronological record of the client's presenting problems. Particular attention is given to stimuli that were acting on the client in the problem situation. Next, factors aggravating or ameliorating responses are identified. A third concern is the social learning contingencies that have influenced the client's development. Here, Wolpe and Lazarus (1966) suggest that the following be explored:

(1) The Family Environment: The focus is on the interaction between the client and significant others, means of discipline and punishment, economic conditions, and religious background.

(2) The Educational Environment: This analysis examines attitudes and experiences (academic and athletic) at all educational levels. In addition, relationships with authority figures, peers, and juniors are reviewed.

(3) The Neighborhood: Here data on interactions with peers, significant friendships, and situations of threat are collected.

(4) The Occupational Environment: This category focuses on the congeniality of employment, relationships with superiors and peers, and the handling of subordinates.

Wolpe and Lazarus (1966) also suggest that the history of the client's sex life be traced from his first awareness of sexual feelings to his current mode of response. In general, the information gathered is used to define a client's problem and the treatment process. An attempt is made to collect behavioral data that is relevant to the client's problem behavior. The analysis focuses on the client's psychological functions.

Kanfer and Saslow (1965) (1969, pp. 417–444) present a similar guide to a functional analysis of individual behavior. They have developed an outline which attempts to provide a working model for the analysis of client behavior. The following is a summary of the categories in the outline:

(1) Analysis of Problem Situation: Here the client's major complaints are categorized into classes of behavioral excesses and deficits. The dimensions of frequency, intensity, duration, appropriateness of form, and stimulus conditions are described for each excess or deficit. The response categories represent the primary targets of the therapeutic intervention.

(2) Clarification of the Problem Situation: In this category the focus is

on the people and circumstances which seem to maintain the disruptive behaviors, and the consequences of these behaviors.

(3) Motivational Analysis: The establishment of a hierarchy of persons, events, and objects which serve as reinforcers for each client is noted. This includes reinforcing events which facilitate approach behaviors as well as those which prompt avoidance responses.

(4) Developmental Analysis: Here behavioral data is collected on the individual's biological attributes, his sociocultural experiences, and his characteristic behavioral development.

(5) Analysis of Self-Control: This section focuses on the methods and the degree of self-control (internal inhibition) exercised by the client in his daily life. Persons, experiences, or institutions that have reinforced self-controlling behavior are reviewed.

(6) Analysis of Social Relationships: The client's social network is investigated in order to assess the impact and significance of the people in the client's environment who may have some effect on the inappropriate behaviors.

(7) Analysis of the Social-Cultural-Physical Environment: In this section the client's behavior is compared to the norms of his natural environment. Agreements and discrepancies between the client's behavior patterns and the norms in the environment are reviewed.

The formulation is action-oriented in that it attempts to define a client's problem in a manner which suggests specific treatment operations (Kanfer and Saslow, 1965; 1969). The categories attempt to focus on variables affecting the client's current behavior.

BEHAVIOR ANALYSIS FOR COUNSELING

Based on the frame of reference used in this book, assessment focuses on the collection of behavioral data to aid in the counseling process as well as to facilitate the learning of new behavior. Consistent with this focus are Ferster's topographic and functional analysis. The topographic analysis, as previously mentioned, attempts to describe the behavioral sequence and the behavioral performance. However, the identification of the behavior by observation or recording alone does not include other relevant data. Whether a student who is exhibiting below average academic performance has a personal problem or is merely performing at the level of his potential is difficult to determine from his behavior only. The relation of his behavior to antecedent conditions and/or events in the past or present environment is certainly a relevant variable. Therefore, a topographic analysis is not sufficient for a thorough understanding of behavior. A functional analysis is necessary to investigate the meaning of the performance. This analysis involves collecting data on antecedent conditions and the relation of behavioral performance to environment. Thus, a need is evident for a framework for a functional analysis of behavior in counseling. Such a framework already exists in the work of Wolpe and Lazarus (1966) and Kanfer and Saslow (1965; 1969). In the following section the framework suggested by these investigators has been adapted to make it especially well suited to the counseling context appropriate to this book.

Problem behavior

In a way similar to Kanfer and Saslow (1965), this effort focuses on the client's major complaints. The complaints are analyzed in terms of excesses and deficits in client coping behaviors. Kanfer and Saslow (1969) have discussed behavioral excesses, deficits, and assets in behavioral terms. To their discussion may be added the impact of the notion of coping responses. Coping responses are significantly involved in the counseling process. Coping behavior refers to the individual's ability to manipulate previously acquired responses to contend with a range of stimuli under varied conditions. The individual generalizes previously acquired responses to new situations. He may also create and implement new coping behaviors in different environments. To some extent, however, these behaviors are affected by previously acquired responses.

In regard to troublesome behaviors, a coping behavior excess is an overt response that occurs frequently in a number of situations, but which is labeled inappropriate because of the high frequency of its occurrence. It may represent too much of a good thing. The behavior may be effective in resolving certain difficulties until engaged in excessively, at which time some undesirable side effects may be seen. Studying hard and long is good up to a point, but carried to an extreme can lead to unrealistic self demands, or social inexperience. A coping behavior deficit occurs when the individual fails to emit or has not learned a specific adaptive response which is acceptable and/or required by a given environment. Both coping behavioral excesses and deficits may have either a cognitive-instrumental or an affective-instrumental basis. Some of the dimensions of behavior suggested by Kanfer and Saslow (1965); (1969), such as frequency, intensity, duration, and appropriateness of form are relevant to the question of behavioral excesses and deficits. To these may be added a description of stimulus conditions under which each excess or deficit occurs. Variation is another dimension which may be used to describe coping behavior excesses. An attempt should be made to identify mediating responses (cognitive and affective) that may be related to an instrumental response deficit sequence. Finally, adequate functional coping behaviors need to be identified.

For example, an 18-year-old male college freshman has been performing

below average academically. The young man has not had sufficient opportunity to learn the adaptive response of study skills (coping behavior) in
the academic environment. Therefore, his instrumental behavioral deficit
stems primarily from a limitation of experience. The behaviors involved
in adequate study activity for this client are infrequent, weak, of short
duration, inappropriate, unrewarding, and are variable and inconsistent.

The problem situation

In this area, coping behavior excesses and deficits are specifically described.
The analysis focuses on stimulus conditions, significant others, and the
environments associated with the occurrence of coping behavior excesses
and deficits. An attempt should be made to identify the satisfactions or
partial reinforcements derived from the behavior excesses or deficits.

Here again we will use the example of the 18-year-old male college
freshman who has the behavioral deficit in the area of study skills. Upon
further investigation, it is learned that the student is a commuter and that
significant others (brother and girl friend) in his environment are having
academic problems. In addition, the home environment is not conducive to
study and the parents in general tend to think college is a waste of time.
However, in high school the client's academic performance (above average)
was rewarding even though (and maybe partly because) it required a
minimum of preparation. Currently he becomes moderately depressed when
he performs below average on an examination. Therefore, an important
satisfaction to him in the past has been successful academic performance.

Work environment

Here the client's environment is considered and compared to his response
repertoire in order to assess the behavioral potential of the environment.
The comparison serves to identify response deficits that the environment
permits and response excesses that the environment is unable to permit.
Next, hierarchies of reinforcing stimuli (persons, events, and objects) that
facilitate approach behavior, and hierarchies of aversive reinforcing stimuli
(Kanfer and Saslow, 1969) that produce avoidance responses should be
identified for the client. This includes significant others, events, and objects
that are associated with and serve to maintain problem behavior (excesses
or deficits) in the work or educational situation. Last, an examination is
made of the client's self-controlling elements in the environment. Self-control
deficits and excesses are to be reviewed as well as events that serve to reinforce
these behaviors.

To continue with the example of the poorly performing student, the
observation can be made that the environment permits, and even requires,

the acquisition of adaptive studying behaviors. In continuing the analysis, certain events that facilitate approach behavior (acquiring study behaviors) may be identified. This hierarchy includes the following:

1. Previous academic reinforcement (earning some above average grades in high school and a consequent feeling of satisfaction);
2. A composite score of 80 on the American College Test Examination;
3. The friendliness of the high school guidance counselor—he has suggested that the client possesses the ability to complete college;
4. The Client's aspiration to participate in college basketball;
5. Earning a grade of A in college algebra;
6. The client's adviser's encouragement to continue college and to seek help;
7. The availability of financial aid.

Similarly a hierarchy of aversive reinforcing stimuli is developed, which includes:

1. Low grades on examinations;
2. Being placed on probation after the first semester;
3. Being required to drop basketball because of his low grades;
4. Being advised to leave college by the professor of his first English course.

Family environment

The client's family relationships are examined in order to evaluate the significance of family members in the client's problem behaviors. First, individuals in the family environment who influence the client's coping behavior excesses or deficits are identified. Then, in the family environment as in the others, it is useful to compare the client's response repertoire to the behavioral potential of the environment. In addition, the hierarchy of reinforcing stimuli, the hierarchy of aversive stimuli, and self-controlling behavior should be developed and examined (Kanfer and Saslow, 1969).

In analyzing the behavior of our student the observation may be made that the family environment does not support the acquisition of study behavior. Instead pressure exists for the client to get a job in order to assume a portion of the financial responsibility at home. The hierarchy of reinforcing stimuli includes the following:

1. The brother's desire to obtain a college degree;
2. The family doctor's encouragement to the client to continue college.

The hierarchy of aversive stimuli includes:

1. The fact that the parents do not value college;
2. The academic problems faced by the brother;
3. The unsuitability of the home environment for studying;
4. The lack of financial aid from home received by the client.

The analysis of the interpersonal environment

This analysis involves the collection of data on peer (male and female) and significant other relationships in order to assess the importance of individuals in the client's social environment who influence his problem behaviors. Generally, this analysis should include an examination of the client's current sexual behavior. Here, again, the client's response repertoire is compared to the behavioral potential of the social environment in order to identify response deficits and excesses that the environment is or is not capable of permitting. Last, the hierarchy of reinforcing stimuli, the hierarchy of aversive stimuli, and self controlling behaviors exhibited in the social environment are listed and evaluated (Kanfer and Saslow, 1969).

In our example the social environment permits the acquisition of study behaviors. No other behavioral excesses or deficits are troublesome in this environment. The hierarchy of reinforcing stimuli in the social environment include the following:

1. The client's girlfriend values a college education;
2. The high school basketball coach is encouraging the client to persist in college;
3. The peer group that the client interacts with values a college education.

The hierarchy of aversive stimuli includes:

1. No financial aid in the community;
2. Friends of the parents in the community do not value higher education.

Thinking process

The client's verbal self-report of his past experiences, problem behavior, work and family environment, social and sexual relationships, and biological functioning, although of unknown validity, provides behavioral data about the client's perceptions of self and environment. In addition, these self-reports may be compared with behavioral data collected from other sources.

Analysis of biological and physical attributes

This topic examines the client's current biological functioning and his recreational responses. Data is collected that does or does not support the assertion of sound and continued biological health. The review also collects data on the client's current physical plan and behavior.

The results of a current physical examination are of value in this analysis. Also, behavioral data may potentially be collected from people the client interacts with during recreation.

The above outline is a potential guide for the collection of behavioral data that will aid in the counseling process. This framework emphasizes the psychological, social, and when data are available, the biological variables, that require examination. After collection the behavioral data are synthesized, collated, and used to determine the treatment process most likely to effectively manipulate the environment, change a specific set of behaviors, or some combination of the two. In general, the focus of this approach is on the client's present environment, his current behavior, and his functioning in the environment. An attempt is made to collect behavioral data about the client in reference to his environment and significant others in his environment.

METHODS FOR THE COLLECTION OF BEHAVIORAL DATA

The previously mentioned guide for the collection of behavioral data indicates the need for new and different methods to be used in data collection. Traditional approaches to data collection include information acquired by means of the client's verbal self-report, observation of his nonverbal behavior, and the collection of psychological test data. However, these methods collect only a modicum of data about the client's behavior in relationship to varying environmental conditions. Therefore, the need exists for methods that will permit the collection of behavioral data about the client in reference to his environment in general and to significant others in the environment in particular.

In the traditional interview the accuracy of a subject's verbal description of his own nonverbal behavior usually is open to question unless it can be independently substantiated. Verbal self-report hardly seems to be sufficient for behavioral analysis and for the prediction of the individual's daily behavior, yet it is relatively rare to find counselors who question client self-report and few instruments exist which try to take client subjective distortions into account.

Two recent investigations (Walsh, 1967; 1968) studied the accuracy of the interview, the questionnaire, and a personal data blank for collecting data which are verifiable. In those studies, self-reported data generally showed evidence of validity under varied conditions (social and financial) for biographical information (grade point average, courses failed, academic probation, A-courses, courses withdrawn from, etc.). In the above two studies, validity was defined as congruence of self-report with an objective independent source of information. The validation process consisted of determining the agreement between interview data and questionnaire data with official university records.

Other studies have focused on more subjective behaviors by attempting to relate test scores and specific criterion behavior, a relationship which is usually ambiguous, if not unknown. Azrin et al. (1961) investigated self-reported fear symptoms during aerial combat and concluded that questionnaire responses may be independent of the actual overt behavior being studied. Geer (1966) observed the relationship between self-reported fears and the Fear Survey Schedule in one study, and in another (Geer, 1965), self-reports of fears and other independent measures of fear behaviors. He used as subjects individuals who were either high in fear of spiders and low in fear of snakes, or who were low in both spider and snake fear. Subjects were shown slides and after each one an autonomic arousal response was given by the subjects who were afraid of spiders, to pictures of spiders. To Geer, the result suggests that the subjects responded to the feared stimuli with increased emotional arousal. Lanyon and Manosevitz (1966) investigated the relationship between a self-report fear measure and several measures of fear made in the fear-arousing situation. Their results suggest that subjects can be assessed on gross levels of fear by means of paper and pencil self-report instruments in the absence of feared stimuli.

In general, there is limited experimental evidence of the specific relationship between a subject's verbal self-report and his nonverbal behavior. Therefore, the client's verbal self-report is not really satisfactory for a behavioral analysis. However, a number of other potential methods for the collection of behavioral data have been cited by various authors (Kanfer and Saslow, 1965; 1969; McDaniel, 1966; Wolpe and Lazarus, 1966). McDaniel (1966) suggests that data about the student in his total ecology be gathered. Some approaches for collecting such data would include measured aptitudes, achievement (tests and grades), teacher descriptions of student activity, parent descriptions of home activity, reports on non-school experiences, data from trained observers and camera, and students' self-report on goals, plans, and problems. McDaniel sees a need for the development of inventories to assess specific behaviors which contribute to or detract from effective learning.

Some methods suggested by Wolpe and Lazarus (1966) include information obtained from family members—friends, employers, and associates. In addition, they suggest that the client respond to a Life History Questionnaire followed by discussion of the responses by the counselor and client. The short Clark-Thurstone inventory now known as Willoughby's Neuroticism Schedule (Willoughby, 1934) may yield important information regarding the client's reactions in some commonly encountered stimulus situations. Also, the client's response to a fear survey (Wolpe and Lang, 1964) may yield significant data on a wide range of disturbed reactions in a short time. Other tests they suggest that may yield important information are the Bernreuter Self-sufficiency Scale, the Maudsley Personality Inventory, and the Eysenck Personality Inventory.

Kanfer and Saslow (1965; 1969) emphasize the importance of describing the client's behavior in relationship to varying environmental conditions.

For example, observations of interactions with significant others can be used in examining variations in the frequency of occurrence of certain behaviors or provide a basis for drawing inferences about the nature of a client's interpersonal relationship with an individual important to him. Confrontation with tape recordings for comparisons between the client's report and the actual experience as witnessed by the observer may provide relevant information. Also, a recording of the client's reaction to the confrontation may be useful in clarifying the client's behavior toward others. Other informants may yield relevant behavioral data if interpersonal problems extend to areas in which social contacts are not clearly defined. Observation of the client's academic or work behavior may produce important information. The client himself may be able to provide samples of his own behavior under different conditions by using a tape recorder for the recording of segments of interactions in his family, at work, or other situations. Kanfer and Saslow suggest that psychological tests may be treated as a miniature life experience, yielding information about variation in the client's behavior as a function of the nature of the stimulus conditions. For a more comprehensive review of the work currently being done by these investigators, see Kanfer and Saslow (1969).

In order to describe the client's behavior in relation to varying environmental conditions the counselor must broaden his sources of observation. Therefore, the counselor need not limit himself to interview data and test data. He must attempt to implement other methods in order to collect behavioral data outside of the interview office. One alternative is the development of a behavioral laboratory which focuses on the assessment of the client's response capabilities. In the laboratory the client would be given the opportunity to perform specific behavioral tasks that he reports being able to perform. For example, if the client perceives and reports that he has a high need for nurturance, an attempt would be made to determine whether or not he makes nurturant behavioral responses (e.g., helping an individual that has dropped his books in the hall). If he reports that he is able to dance, the client should be given the opportunity to implement the behavior. Other response capabilities that could be assessed are client affiliation, cooperation, work behavior, order, dominance, deference, verbal facility, writing ability, study skills, occupational information for a specific position, etc.

Holland (1965) has developed and used several non-academic accomplishment scales that would seem to be valuable methods of collecting behavioral data. The Extracurricular Achievement Record (Holland and Nichols, 1964), a checklist of extracurricular accomplishment for the high school years, may be used to obtain scores in art, music, literature, dramatic arts, leadership, and science. For example, science items included accomplishments such as: did an independent scientific experiment; placed first, second, or third in a national contest; etc. Leadership items included:

appointed to a student office; organized own business or service; etc. The items on the other scales consisted of similar content and planned to assess a range of achievement. Students with high scores on one or more of these scales have attained a high level of accomplishment which generally received public recognition so that such accomplishments can probably be verified. In general, the scale scores and item responses to this checklist would be useful behavioral information about the client's non-academic accomplishments.

On the Range of Competencies (Holland, 1965) students checked those activities from a list of 143 which "you can do well or competently." The assumption underlying these scales is that a large number of competencies in an area is conducive to achievement in that area. Some items from this list are: I can dance, I am a good cook, I can read Greek, I can use logarithm tables, etc. The number of activities checked equals the individual's range of competencies. This activity checklist could potentially yield relevant behavioral data some of which could be verified in a behavioral laboratory.

The Interpersonal Competency Scale (Holland, 1965) was modeled after the work of Foote and Cottrell (1955), who defined interpersonal competence as "acquired ability for effective interaction." The scale items assess those factors that Foote and Cottrell believe to be conducive to interpersonal competency-good health, social experience, competencies, and positive self-regard.

Behavioral data on a client's academic performance in a college environment would be reflected by his grade point average and performance on standardized measures of educational achievement. In addition, the client's response to an instrument such as the Study Skills Diagnostic Inventory (Campbell, 1966) may yield important behavioral data concerning study behavior. The purpose of this inventory is to help the client identify ineffective study habits and to become aware of effective study behaviors. The inventory yields the twelve following scales: general attitudes and motivation to study; reading skills and techniques; efficient use of time; preparation for exams and tests; classroom skills; examination skills; study concentration skills; writing reports and themes; ruminative; compulsive; study avoidance; and performance.

Behavioral data about a client's interests may be acquired by observing the client's manifest interests as well as the more common practice of assessing his expressed and inventoried interests. Manifest interest is assessed by observing an individuals' participation in an activity or occupation (Super and Crites, 1962). Thus, manifest interest implies to a degree a commitment to an occupational area because of the individual's direct involvement in the work activity. This is not to say that the high school youth who was active in the dramatic club will have artistic or literary interests. However, the fact that he was active in such a club may provide useful information about antecedent conditions and his behavior in a similar situation.

An examination of tested interests may also produce significant behavioral data. Tested interests are measured by objective tests (Super and Crites, 1962). It is thought that since interest in an activity is likely to result in relevant overt action, the outcome should be an accumulation of general information about the activity involved. Therefore, interest in science should lead a person to read about scientific developments and acquire more information about science than would other people. Some attempts have been made to construct interest tests. Greene (1940) developed the Michigan Vocabulary Profile to measure interest through specialized vocabularies. The Cooperative Test Service constructed a general information test which measures interests in several areas. During World War II the General Information Test was developed which produced differential scores for pilots, navigators, and bombardiers. This test proved to be the most valid test in the Air Force's selection battery (Flanagan, 1946; DuBois, 1947).

The construction of an experience inventory that would assess the range and breadth of the client's response repertoire may be a useful method of collecting behavioral data. The client would be asked to report previous responses and experiences under different conditions. Some potential items are: I have opened a bank account; I purchase my own clothing; I play softball; I read Time magazine; I read Playboy magazine; I have had sexual intercourse; etc. In general, the past experiences and responses of a client are relevant because they help him make judgments about and engage in behaviors leading to the completion of various tasks.

Client responses to the Adjective Check List (Gough and Heilbrun, 1965) may yield useful data. An individual's self-description may tell us something about his overt behavior. The ACL has 24 scales, 15 of which are need scales. The need scales to some extent reflect the client's pattern of overt behavior. In using the ACL one should examine the specific adjectives checked by the client. For example, if a client checks the adjectives hostile, bitter and quarrelsome, this information would seem to tell us something about his behavior.

Behavioral analysis is potentially useful in counselor supervision. Osipow and Walsh (1968) recently developed a Counselor Rating Scale to be used to assess specific counselor behaviors by the supervisor. The supervisor may then discuss the behavior ratings with the counselor, providing specific behavioral feedback to the neophyte counselor. The scale may be used to obtain scores in the following areas: counselor communication skills; counselor understanding of client; helps client with problems; counselor sensitivity; and a general area. For example, the counselor understanding of client area includes items such as: able to tell client when he fails to understand client; counselor is thorough; counselor develops suitable objectives; hypotheses developed by the counselor seem valid under scrutiny; etc. This scale is currently an experimental research instrument but shows promise for the measurement of specific counselor behavior, and for the evaluation of the impact of specific counselor behaviors on client behavioral patterns.

In general, the above methods and those presented by Kanfer and Saslow (1965; 1969), MacDaniel (1966), and Wolpe and Lazarus (1966) show potential for the gathering of behavioral data under varied environment conditions. However, a need exists for the construction of specific inventories to measure specific behaviors which contribute to the development of effective learning under varied conditions.

BEHAVIOR ANALYSIS AND COUNSELING STRATEGIES

The techniques of analysis presented in this chapter, plus elaborations of these techniques yet to be developed, should permit a thorough understanding of client behavior, problems, strengths, weaknesses, and environmental supports. Once the analysis has been completed, the application of the understanding into useful counseling procedures remains. In the next chapter a number of counseling strategies will be presented. The information collected and analyzed through the procedures just described should lead logically to one or some combination of the strategies. The potential adequacy of each strategy to deal effectively with the client's concerns lies in the accuracy with which the data collected and analyzed are appraised.

SUMMARY

The purpose of this chapter was to develop a taxonomy for behavioral data and to consider methods of collecting behavioral data. A major contribution has been Ferster's (1965) classification of behavior into static (topographic analysis) and dynamic (functional analysis) factors. Like Ferster, Bijou (1965) proposed a shift in the diagnostic procedure from the current practice of the identification of psychological traits to an analysis of psychological functions.

In a review of potential dimensions of a behavior analysis Wolpe and Lazarus (1966) suggest that a chronological record of the client's presenting problems be developed, the factors aggravating or ameliorating responses be identified, and that the social learning contingencies that have influenced development be identified. Kanfer and Saslow (1965; 1969), presenting a guide to a functional analysis of individual behavior, suggest a number of behavioral categories: analysis of the problem situation, clarification of the problem situation, motivational analysis, developmental analysis, analysis of self-control, analysis of social relationships, and analysis of the social-cultural-physical environment.

In the frame of reference presented in this book, assessment means the collection of behavioral data to aid in the counseling process as well as to facilitate the learning of new behavior. Consistent with this focus are Ferster's two factors—topographic analysis and functional analysis. In order to aid the counselor in the collection and organization of information in a behavioral analysis the following outline was presented: problem behavior, problem situation, work environment, family environment, interpersonal relationships, thinking process, and biological and physical attributes.

The above mentioned guide for the collection of behavioral data indicates the need for new and different methods to be used in data collection. Potential methods for the collection of behavioral data were cited and discussed (Kanfer and Saslow, 1965; 1969; McDaniel, 1966; Wolpe and Lazarus, 1966).

REFERENCES

Azrin, N. H., Holz, D., and Goldiamond, I. Response bias in questionnaire reports. *Journal of Consulting Psychology*, 1961, *25*, 324-326.

Bijou, S. W. Implications of behavioral science for counseling and guidance. In Krumboltz, J. D. (Ed.), *Revolution in counseling*. Boston: Houghton-Mifflin, 1966.

Campbell, R. E. A diagnostic study skills inventory. Paper presented at American Personnel and Guidance Association, Washington, D.C., 1966.

DuBois, P. H. (Ed.) The classification program. AAF Aviation Psychology Report No. 2, Washington, D.C.: U.S. Government Printing Office, 1947.

Ferster, C. B. Classification of behavioral pathology. In Krasner, L. and Ullman, L. P. (Eds.) *Research in behavior modification*. New York: Holt, Rinehart, and Winston, 1965.

Flanagan, J. C. The experimental evaluation of a selection procedure. *Educational and Psychological Measurement*, 1946, *6*, 445-466.

Foote, N. N. and Cottrell, L. S. *Identity and interpersonal competencies*. Chicago: University of Chicago, 1955.

Geer, J. The development of a scale to measure fear. *Behavior Research and Therapy*, 1965, *3*, 45-53.

Geer, J. Fear and autonomic arousal. *Journal of Abnormal Psychology*, 1966, *71*, 253-255.

Gough, H. G. and Heilbrun, A. B. *The adjective checklist manual*. Palo Alto, California, Consulting Psychologists Press, 1965.

Greene, E. B. Vocabulary profiles of groups in training. *Journal of Educational Research*, 1940, *33*, 569-575.

Holland, J. L. and Nichols, R. C. Prediction of academic and extracurricular achievement in college. *Journal of Educational Psychology*, 1964, *55*, 55-65.

Holland, J. L. and Richards, J. M., Jr. Academic and non-academic accomplishment: correlated or uncorrelated? American College Testing Program, Research Report No. 2, 1965.

Kanfer, F. H. and Saslow, G. Behavioral analysis: an alternative to diagnostic classification. *Archives of General Psychiatry*, 1965, *12*, 529-538.

Kanfer, F. H. and Saslow, G. Behavioral diagnosis. In Franks, C. (Ed.) *Assessment and status of the behavior therapies and associated developments*. New York: McGraw-Hill, 1969, pp. 417-444.

Krasner, L. and Ullmann, L. P. An introduction to research in behavior modification. In Krasner, L. and Ullmann, L. P. (Eds.), *Research in behavior modification*. New York: Holt, Rinehart, and Winston, 1965.

Lanyon, R. I. and Manosevitz, M. Validity of self-reported fear. *Behavioral Research and Therapy*. 1966, *4*, 259-263.

McDaniel, H. B. Counseling perspectives: old and new. In Krumboltz, J. D. (Ed.), *Revolution in counseling.* Boston: Houghton-Mifflin, 1966.

Osipow, S. H. and Walsh, W. B. A behavioral rating scale for judging counselor performance (Experimental Form 2). Columbus, Ohio: Department of Psychology, Ohio State University, 1968.

Peterson, D. R. *The clinical study of social behavior.* N.Y.: Appleton-Century-Crofts, 1968.

Super, D. E. and Crites, J. O. *Appraising vocational fitness.* (Revised Edition) New York: Harper, 1962.

Walsh, W. B. Validity of self-report. *Journal of Counseling Psychology,* 1967, *14,* 18-23.

Walsh, W. B. Validity of self-report: another look. *Journal of Counseling Psychology,* 1968, *15,* 180-186.

Willoughby, R. R. Norms for the Clark-Thurstone Inventory. *Journal of Social Psychology,* 1934, *5,* 91-97.

Wolpe, J. and Lang, P. J. A fear survey schedule for use in behavior therapy. *Behavior Research and Therapy,* 1964, *2,* 27-30.

Wolpe, J. and Lazarus, A. A. *Behavior therapy techniques.* New York: Pergamon Press, 1966.

Chapter 4

Counseling Strategies

It has commonly been the practice to classify counseling problems according to similarities exhibited by the clients, especially as these similarities are related to the content aspects of the clients' difficulties. Some theoretical approaches to counseling assume that client difficulties represent symptoms which reflect some basic malfunction. Often, one, or a few, kinds of malfunctions are seen to underlie a wide range of problems. The result is the development of a single counseling style to deal with all, or at least a very wide range, of client concerns (e.g., the client-centered approach). An alternative is to ask "what are the antecedent or concurrent conditions responsible for. . . efficiency in problem solving, vocational choice, avoidant behavior. . ." (Sarbin, 1968). Certainly, there seems to be a need to move in the direction of emphasizing behavior change rather than psychic change (Gardner, 1967). Some research findings (Paul, 1966; 1967) suggest the likelihood that differences exist in the effectiveness of various kinds of interview treatments with different problem behaviors. Evidence is accumulating to suggest that client problems are differentially effected by treatments of various kinds (e.g., Ford and Urban, 1963; Allen et al, 1968; Paul, 1966).

The interventionistic-cognitive approach attends to the specification of the behavioral goals for both the client and the counselor. This combination allows the IC counselor to be effective with a wide variety of cases as far as problem content is concerned. For convenience, four kinds of cases and strategies have been identified: those emphasizing the supportive role of the counselor, those in which the counselor's main efforts are directed toward client behavior acquisition and/or modification, those requiring the client to arrive at major specific decisions, and problems involving client deficiencies in crucial vocational or scholastic skills. The distinction between the behavior acquisition-modification and skill deficiency strategies is more one of convenience than concept.

SUPPORTIVE CASES

General Characteristics. The type of case in which the supportive role is adopted as the principle strategy is generally characterized by a heavy situational component. These situational factors might be seen in a student's agitation over his failure to handle an academic load effectively, the distress felt over a disrupted love affair, concern over temporary financial strain, marital difficulties that seem to stem from transient situational events, grief reaction in response to the death or enforced and prolonged absence of a loved one, or a depression following a significant failure in life. The key is thus the counselor's recognition that the principle antecedents are temporary, common to human experience, and largely beyond the power of the client to control.

The supportive approach may logically be taken under a second set of conditions. When the client's difficulties are so pervasive that the counselor finds it difficult or impossible to identify accurately and/or deal with the antecedents, a practical objective of counseling is to help the client deal with the situational components of his distress in the hope that further deterioration can be avoided. In effect, the strategy is adopted at times when no other approach seems cogent. At times, a case approached in a supportive way for this reason will develop in such a manner that more positive possibilities occur, and the supportive phase of the case may, retrospectively, be seen as having contributed to the client's readiness for working more directly on his problems and effecting greater behavioral changes.

The goals of supportive counseling are limited, in accordance with the temporary nature of the difficulties. No major behavior changes are expected. Rather, the termination of certain behavior sequences might be seen as the primary objective. The student agitated over his academic load would be led to engage in behaviors which allow him to avoid the deleterious effects of panic, the jilted lover or grieving mother would be helped to develop behaviors instrumental to the inhibition of their grief, the arguing spouses would be helped to inhibit the expression of inappropriate aggression. In fact, the goals may be seen as helping the client to avoid engaging in behavior which adds to his woes and thus leads to more permanent distress while waiting for the transient and self-limiting affective behaviors to run their course. Except in what may be considered to be pathological states, the emotions of grief, depression, anxiety, and worry, seem to be self-limiting, and terminate or at least moderate, after the emotional response has reached a certain level of intensity and duration.

At the same time, the counselor might hope to help the client to develop more effectiveness in the use of already existing instrumental responses that might materially deal with his problem. Considering the two kinds of objectives and the context within which supportive counseling would occur, these cases would not ordinarily be expected to be of long duration; more commonly requiring short term but frequent counseling sessions; possibly two or three extended sessions a week for a few weeks.

Counselor behavior. The proper role for the counselor to play in using the supportive approach is to ally himself with the client so the client does not feel his isolation with the problem as acutely as before counseling. The counselor can use the alliance to encourage mildly (or reinforce), and thus accelerate, client behaviors that naturally terminate the troublesome responses or indicate the incipient presence of useful instrumental behaviors. Initially, the counselor responds minimally, encouraging the client to ventilate his concerns. The counselor responds in a way that communicates his understanding and regard to the client. The counselor strives to elicit client verbal behaviors that lead to the client's finding new ways to handle his difficulty. Later, as the need for support becomes less intense, the counselor might help the client to improve some already existing skills that would be useful in dealing with the troublesome behaviors, perhaps help the client manage his affairs to put them back into order after letting them go during his distress. At times, the counselor might help the client at this stage by intervention and situational manipulation to allow him to pick up the threads of his life. For example, he might help one student make a change of academic objective, help another student explain a failure to a punitive parent, or suggest membership in a social club to a lonely, grieving young woman.

DECISION-MAKING CASES

A great amount of the counseling activity in educational settings is concerned with client decision-making. Either the client is confronted with an environmental demand to reach a decision with perceived, far reaching implications, or the client has already decided what he wishes to do, but wants confirmation, or assistance in taking steps to implement his decision. The antecedents of a client's decision-making difficulties determine the strategy most appropriate to use (Ashby, Wall, and Osipow, 1966).

The goal, obviously, of such casework is the successful implementation of the decision. Since the "correctness" of most decisions is not immediately obvious, and in some instances not known for years, it is not reasonable to maintain the objective of counseling at so abstract a plane. Consequently, numerous sub-goals are appropriately identified in working with decision-making cases. For example, an appropriate set of goals in working with a college freshman might be the planning of a schedule of courses to take for a quarter, for the sophomore it might include the selection of a college major, while for the senior it would probably involve the selection of one of several job offers. It should be noted that the selection of a major, scheduling of courses, and the acceptance of a job offer do not necessarily commit the individual to a definite future course of action beyond that which immediately follows the choice. In a way, it may be seen as one aspect of the exploratory process, since majors may be changed, schedules revised, and jobs quit.

Even more molecular sub-goals for counseling are often appropriate in working with decision-making cases. As Krumboltz and his associates have demonstrated in several studies (Krumboltz and Schroeder, 1965; Krumboltz and Thoreson, 1964; Krumboltz, Varenhorst, and Thoreson, 1967; Ryan and Krumboltz, 1964) one kind of behavioral goal in counseling is the development of specific behaviors designed to collect decision related information or facilitate exploration. Academic schedules can at times be planned specifically to explore several scholastic possibilities systematically. Automated approaches to occupational information (Campbell, Tiedeman, and Martin, 1966) are also procedures which might be employed to increase the range of the client's vicarious experience.

Clients who consult counselors for help in making decisions are often somewhat more direct in their presentation of their concerns than are those who may need the supportive or behavior modification-acquisition approaches. Clients needing help with decisions will present problems such as the following: they complain of an inability to make up their mind about an academic major, or they can't decide which job offer to accept, or what courses to schedule. For the counselor, the first step to be taken in decision-making counseling is to make more explicit the decision that must be made. Not infrequently, clients extrapolate from current decisions to future ones, unnecessarily complicating the problem by compounding various sets of decisions. In other words, it is a far different matter to decide upon a college major than a first position in what is perceived to be a career ladder. For example, at college entrance students are faced with the decision of enrolling in a science or non-science program, which is very different from being required to specify a major or select a career. Yet, many students act as if the two were equivalent. Much overlap between the two exists, but many chances for the modification of plans between the college major and first job exist, and plans will or will not be modified as a function of feedback that will result following the student's experience with his newly chosen major.

The Dollard and Miller (1950) formulation of the implication of the approach-avoidance gradient on behavior is relevant. Such questions as the desirable features of an engineering curriculum (prestige, apparent job security, good income) lead a student to consider engineering to the point where the avoidant aspects (hard studying, long hours in class and lab, inability to study many electives, fear of failure) begin to loom larger. Counseling procedures for the above approach-avoidance conflict might be very different from those to be followed in an avoidance-avoidance, or approach-approach situation.

After the required decision becomes clearer, attention may be given to the identification of realistic alternatives open to the client. Here it sometimes becomes apparent that the range of responses open to the client may preclude much choice, in which case the object of the counseling is to help the client develop behaviors that will either expand the range of choices possible or live more comfortably within his restricted range of alternatives. It may become apparent that the client has tried to reach a decision prematurely out of a desire to reduce anxiety resulting from an ambiguous situation. Thus, the college freshman may feel a strong concern over the choice of his life's work because not knowing distracts him from his studies. Yet choosing as a freshman is inefficient since the student has yet to encounter many stimuli relevant to his occupational selection. The objective of counseling is to help the client develop behaviors contributing to more effective living under the conditions of ambiguity imposed by necessary and temporary indecisiveness. A further purpose is to develop planning behaviors which contribute to the client's occupational decision that must be made later. The latter will probably reduce client anxiety somewhat since it can be perceived as a set of behaviors aimed at dealing with a problem.

Where the choice alternatives identified are numerous and the timing for choice is appropriate, data collection about the alternatives is usually relevant. Thus, test scores, inventories of client behaviors, and information about environmental press will be collected, analyzed, and discussed with the client, with the hope that it will be possible to predict, to some extent, client satisfaction and success likely to be associated with various decisions.

Most commonly, decision-making cases are of relatively short duration, perhaps two to five interviews. However, it may be that individuals who consult professionals at times of major discontinuities in their lives will return for counseling at later times of decision. Thus, the counseling pattern associated with decision-making cases might well be brief, intense, and recurring. An individual might be seen at the outset of a college career, at the end of his sophomore year, and during his senior year. Other counselors in other settings might be consulted when other life choices are to be made.

BEHAVIOR MODIFICATION-ACQUISITION

A third case strategy centers around behavior acquisition and/or modification. The type of situation in which this is most suitable is characterized by the client who complains of ineffectiveness in some behavioral realm, most commonly social or interpersonal, possibly academic or vocational. In this type of case, certain behavior sequences of the client contribute to his failure to accomplish some interpersonal objective or to be less effective in his social relations than he would hope to be. As a result, the problem could be resolved by merely eliminating some behavior sequence of the client (Katahn, 1967) or reducing its frequency or intensity, or by helping the

client to develop some new behavior sequence or sequences, or some combination of the three. The counselor's general goals are to identify the inappropriate behavior, identify appropriate behavior to replace it, and devise a learning program to accomplish the replacement. Many examples of
cases treated this way exist (e.g., Geer and Silverman, 1967; Geer, 1964;
Geer and Katkin, 1966; Ullmann and Krasner, 1965). Procedures specifying
bination of the three. The counselor's general goals are to identify the inappropriate behavior, identity appropriate behavior to replace it, and
devise a learing program to accomplish the replacement. Many examples of
cases treated this way exist (e.g., Geer and Silverman, 1967; Geer, 1964;
Geer and Katkin, 1966; Ullmann and Krasner, 1965). Procedures specifying
the selection and application of consequences might also be employed in
order to manipulate the frequency of occurrence of desired and undesired
behavior (Whelan and Haring, 1966).

As with other kinds of cases, the general goals must be made operational
and concrete. Clients for whom the behavior acquisition-modification procedures are suitable may complain initially of not being able to make friends,
of being timid interpersonally, of encountering numerous interpersonal
conflicts, or of feeling anxious in social situations. For the first client, the
behavioral goals include specific behaviors leading to social interchange,
such as smiling appropriately upon meeting others, social seeking behaviors,
conversational skills, and efforts to remember names and faces of new ac-
quaintances. For the timid, aggressive, and anxious clients, similar goals might
exist, but a prior set of sub-goals would need to be identified first. Certain
behaviors are likely to be occurring which contribute to the client's difficulties and which need to be extinguished before consideration can be given to
the question of adding behaviors to the client's repertoire. For example, the
timid client may be engaging in subjective verbal responses cueing himself to
expect rejection or ridicule. If so, the responses should be made explicit and
conditions arranged to help the client extinguish or reduce these responses.
Perhaps the extinction phase is all that is necessary. In similar ways, the
anxious or aggressive client is likely to be engaging in some private responses which need to be made accessible to the counselor and the client and
extinguished before the second set of behavioral goals, reducing anxiety or
aggressiveness, can be accomplished. In this case the instrumental aspect of
the counseling task occurs after the subjective responses have been identified
and modified. The first sub-set of behavioral goals are related to client talk in
the interview, which should provide the counselor with some information
concerning the parameters of the problem he is working on.

Counselor behavior. To accomplish the objectives just described, the counselor
should appropriately engage in several specific kinds of behaviors. He first
wishes to elicit from the client verbal representations of subjective reactions,
in order to determine what behaviors, if any, need to be extinguished. The

overt aspects of the verbalization make the response accessible to extinction. Engaging the client in behaviors both in and out of the interview which fail to produce expected consequences contributes to the extinction of subjective emotional responses. Thus, the client fearful of social rejection might find that he is not rejected, or that even when he is rejected the events are not nearly as painful as he anticipated.

The counselor is also concerned with the arrangement of learning conditions during which new and appropriate behaviors can be acquired. These new behaviors include both overt instrumental responses as well as covert mediational responses which will both cue and reinforce the client in his new behavior patterns. There is some evidence to suggest that the modification of cognitions about fearful stimuli may contribute to the reduction of avoidant responses made in the presence of the feared object (Valins and Ray, 1967).

Since the counselor wants to take advantage of already existing client responses, the counselor takes pains to elicit useful behaviors from the client to be shaped and brought to bear in acquiring new patterns of more effective responses. Following this, the counselor helps the client identify and arrange conditions for practicing the new patterns of behavior, during which time the counselor provides feedback and coaching to the client.

The interview schedule followed in such a case would be varied. During early periods when the counselor is concerned with eliciting subjective responses from the client, contact might occur for one hour periods once every three or four days. During the phase of elicitation of behaviors to be shaped and arrangement of outside conditions in which to extinguish old and acquire new behaviors, frequent and brief counselor-client contact might be most appropriate. Once the client is operating fairly effectively with his new behaviors, the frequency and length of counselor-client contact would be reduced, tapering off to termination.

PERFORMANCE PROBLEMS

Another kind of client concern which occupies a great deal of the time of the counselor involves difficulties having to do with individual productivity or effectiveness in work related activities. In the student, these problems are seen in poor academic achievement and even failure, often in the face of apparently adequate abilities. Sometimes the difficulties are closely related to poorly conceived goals. In the employed adult, performance problems are reflected in low work output, failure to gain promotion or advancement, and possibly underemployment or unemployment. The general counseling objectives for such cases are closely tied to the performance task itself, and may be illustrated by the following: increase grade point level for the student, reduce the amount of work time necessary to achieve the same level of performance, raise the ratio of time employed to unemployed during the year, increase client earnings, raise job level, etc.

More is known about how to approach these problems in the academic setting than in the work setting since more counselors have devoted attention to scholastic than industrial matters. However, some lessons might be learned from industrial psychologists in terms of helping workers increase their productivity and enhance their job status. In working with the student, three possibilities to account for ineffective performance seem likely. The first is related to the degree to which the student's academic curriculum and objectives are supported by measures of ability, past achievement, and inventorie interests. Students have many reasons behind their academic choices, some of them sound, many of them irrelevant or illogical. At times, academic performance is closely related to the enrollment in an inappropriate academic program because of some misidentified interests or wishful thinking. A student seeking counseling with that kind of background might say things like: "I can't seem to get as interested in my chemistry courses as I should," or, "I really thought engineering would have more to do with making things," or, "I really want to be a social worker, but the courses I have to take in psychology and economics don't seem related to my desire to help people." For such clients, the performance problem may be substantially alleviated by reconceiving the problem as a decision problem, and working along the lines suggested by that strategy to help the client identify a new way to accomplish his goals, or help him modify his goals to reflect his personal attributes more closely.

A second possibility to account for ineffective performance in school stems from the disruptive effect on a student's ability to concentrate that may result from a problem in another sphere of his life, or a preoccupation with some other developmental task which momentarily occupies the major share of the student's attention. Thus, a student might find it hard to concentrate on his calculus course when his parents are in the midst of divorce proceedings, when a parent is dying of cancer, or if he is concerned about earning enough money to keep himself in school from quarter to quarter. For this student the proper approach to counseling would seem to lie in the supportive strategy. Another student might find it difficult to study effectively if he is concerned about his interpersonal skills and preoccupied with thoughts about his social adequacy, or if he is dealing with the heterosexual developmental task and is constantly rehashing his dating activities. For this student, the best approach might stem from the behaviour modification-acquisition strategy.

Both of the above possibilities might mislead the counselor to begin with, because the students might very well begin their initial counseling session by complaining of their poor academic performance, or their inability to concentrate effectively, or their failure to know how to study, or their anxiety over "flunking out". It can be seen, however, that the antecedents to the client complaints lie elsewhere and procedures other than those aimed at improving performance level are likely to be most effective.

Only the third kind of student, the one who genuinely needs help in developing more effective ways of learning, can really be classified as a suitable candidate for the performance strategy. This student, to the best of the counselor's ability to assess, is enrolled in a program consistent with his interests, talents, and achievement, and is not unduly distracted by situational concerns or developmental tasks. He really doesn't know the methods by which he can take notes more effectively, organize various kinds of academic material, study for exams, and so on.

Much of the counselor's task in the performance case is involved in work to assure himself that no antecedent conditions other than techniques are creating the difficulty. Once so assured, the counselor's task is the explication of the failure sequence in behavioral terms, teaching the client to externalize and thus gain operational control over instrumental responses related to studying and reading, and set the client on a retraining schedule during which phase the counselor acts as a coach. (An example of this applied to a young child may be seen in the case described by Allen, 1967.) Once improvement is observed, follow up observations should be made at periodic intervals. The schedule and timing of these intervals might appropriately be frequent and brief at first, occasional and brief later on in the program of improvement. The counselor has as aids a number of study skills texts which may help the client to structure his task of studying (e.g., Robinson, 1961).

In nonacademic settings the task is somewhat different. Here, once again, the counselor must assure himself that other behavior change strategies are not likely to be more effective. Once so convinced, the task becomes one of helping the client identify, in operational terms, those behaviors that will raise his performance level, or specify tasks that are logically connected to promotion. The converse approach is also appropriate, i.e., assessing those behaviors which interfere with successful performance. These might be identified as behaviors which do not contribute to successful performance and contradict desirable instrumental responses. For example, in academia, research and publication is prerequisite for tenure and promotion, and one engages in activities related to those ends if he wishes to advance. Similarly, certain behaviors are likely to lead to advancement for the salesman, the lawyer, the teacher, the skilled tradesman. Not infrequently, the worker is not clearly aware of the instrumental behaviors that will bring him to the ends he desires. At other times he does not come to grips with the "costs" in time and effort that are required to accomplish the advancement he says he desires. The young man employed as a sales clerk who wants to become an "executive" first needs to know what behaviors are necessary to acquire that new status and second, he must decide if he has the capability and desire to engage in these behaviors.

COUNSELING STRATEGIES AND COUNSELING THEORY

The idea of developing strategies for counseling is clearly a move away from approaches to counseling that have been developed from single treatment counseling styles. Generally, counseling theories have been surprisingly narrow in the methods deemed appropriate to bring about change. Most commonly, goals of counseling have been the development of insight and interpersonal relationships. In the IC approach insight disappears as a single entity and is replaced by a more explicit description of behaviors that are judged to reflect "self-understanding." Thus, insight becomes a more useful concept. The development of insight, as such, is not sought. What is sought is the development of a set of behaviors which result in a greater potential for effectiveness.

Similarly, the client-counselor relationship is depicted in operational, behavioral terms, and is construed to be an important vehicle for aiding the client to make certain kinds of behavioral changes (Truax, 1961). Where important to a case strategy, the "relationship" is stressed and polished, but it should not replace the importance of client-oriented behavior change, lest it serve the counselor more than the client. The IC approach to counseling strives to retain the values of introspection translated into more explicit terms. As a result of specifying the behavioral sequence patterns, syndromes, course and effects, and antecedents of subjective client states the counselor hopes to see relationships between events that were not previously apparent. Once these relationships are recognized they are likely to be amenable to counselor intervention through the application of one of the behavioral approaches suggested by Grossberg (1964). Grossberg has named five kinds of behavioral treatment approaches: presentation or elimination of aversive stimuli, negative practice, operant conditioning, reinforcement withdrawal, and desensitization. These procedures are most likely to be used in conjunction with the behavior modification-acquisition and performance strategies.

There is no need to adopt a single strategy and rigidly adhere to it. Leventhal (1968) has described a case which exemplifies the use of multiple counseling strategies. A client was systematically led through a succession of different types of interviews, each designed to deal with an aspect of her problem needing resolution before further progress could be made. Initially, the counselor's approach was reflective and nondirective, at a time when the counselor was concerned with building rapport and confidence. Gradually, the procedure became increasingly interpretive. Finally, a desensitization phase was entered, partly to facilitate client discussion of frightening material and partly to enable her to engage in behavior related to the frightening stimuli outside of the interview.

BEHAVIORAL ASSESSMENT AND COUNSELING STRATEGIES

Some mention must be made of the relationship between behavioral assessment and behavioral analysis, described in Chapter 3, and the determination of the case strategies to be followed in working with a given client. The more precise and specific the behavioral analysis, the more specifically the counselor can determine a program to follow, and the greater the accuracy with which he can predict its effectiveness. Part II, case illustrations, has been written to provide some examples of how these strategies are determined and effected in counseling.

SUMMARY

The approach to counseling espoused in this chapter is built upon the assumption that counseling objectives of different kinds are suitable for various types of client concerns. Further, it takes the position that once the objectives are determined, methods to obtain them will be differentially effective. As a consequence, the assessment of client behavior and objectives discussed in the previous chapter assumes special importance.

However, the viewpoint does not necessarily assume that client objectives and counselor approaches to these objectives are necessarily static. It is very reasonable to assume that as early objectives in a counseling case are successfully accomplished new objectives may be identified which require somewhat different approaches to deal with effectively.

Counselor behaviors, which may cut across the case-types to some extent, primarily emphasize what goes on in the interview itself. These include counselor analysis of behavior sequences and feedback to the client for the purpose of helping the client gain insight into certain of his behaviors, their antecedents, and their consequences. In the interest of establishing that insight, the counselor may use supportive techniques and elicit client talk about his concern in order to help the client "ventilate" his concerns, or he may try to establish a miniature interpersonal relationship in which many of the client's ineffective interpersonal behaviors will become highlighted, and thus open to change. This insight might be useful as an end in itself with respect to certain kinds of client behaviors which are characterized by the individual's ability to bring responses under control easily and directly.

More often, however, the counselor must engage in teaching the client instrumental behaviors which will enable the client effectively to take advantage of the insights he has gathered via the analysis of behavior sequences. The counselor facilitates the acquisition of these instrumental behaviors through the use of a variety of methods, ranging from teaching specific skills to the client, coaching, analyzing and assessing the feedback from the client's efforts to change, and encouraging and reinforcing the client's new behaviors personally.

The counselor's prime concern is the building of bridges between those events that occur in the interview and the critical events in the client's life that occur out of the interview situation. To this end, he helps the client identify and implement situational manipulations, teaches the client to intervene in the stream of events in his own behalf, encourages practice of new and more effective responses in the field, and points to new behaviors the client can try out between interviews, the effects of which may be assessed in subsequent interviews. No matter how improved is the client's talk about his concerns in the interview, what really matters is the degree to which the behavioral goals identified have been achieved.

REFERENCES

Allen, K. Eileen Control of hyperactivity by social reinforcement of attending behaviors. *Journal of Educational Psychology*, 1967, *58*, 231-237.

Allen, T. W., Whiteley, J. M., Sprinthall, N. A., Mosher, R., and Donagby, R. *Dimensions of effective counseling.* Columbus, Ohio: Merrill, 1968.

Ashby, J. D., Wall, H. W. and Osipow, S. H. Vocational certainty and indecision in college freshmen. *Personnel and Guidance Journal*, 1966, *44*, 1037-1041.

Campbell, R. E., Tiedeman, D. V., and Martin, Ann (Eds.) *Systems under development for vocational guidance.* Columbus, Ohio: Center for Vocational and Technical Education, Ohio State University, 1966.

Dollard, J. and Miller, N. E. *Personality and psychotherapy.* New York: McGraw-Hill, 1950.

Ford, D. H. and Urban, H. B. *Systems of psychotherapy.* New York: Wiley, 1963.

Ford, D. H. and Urban, H. B. (Eds.) *Planned behavior change.* Division of Counseling Monograph, University Park, Pennsylvania, 1963.

Gardner, W. I. What should be the psychologist's role? *Mental Retardation*, 1967, *5*, 29-31.

Geer, J. Phobia treated by reciprocal inhibition. *Journal of Abnormal and Social Psychology*, 1964, *69*, 642-645.

Geer, J. and Katkin, E. S. Treatment of insomnia using a variant of systematic desensitization. *Journal of Abnormal Psychology*, 1966, *71*, 161-164.

Geer, J. and Silverman, I. Treatment of recurrent nightmare by behavior modification procedures. *Journal of Abnormal Psychology*, 1967, *72*, 188-190.

Grossberg, J. M. Behavior therapy: a review. *Psychological Bulletin*, 1964, *62*, 77-88.

Katahn, M. Systematic desensitization and counseling for anxiety in a college basketball player. *Journal of Special Education*, 1967, *1*, 309-314.

Krumboltz, J. D. and Schroeder, W. W. Promoting career planning though reinforcement and models. *Personnel and Guidance Journal*, 1965, *44*, 19-26.

Krumboltz, J. D. and Thoreson, C. E. The effect of behavioral counseling in group and individual settings on information-seeking behavior. *Journal of Counseling Psychology*, 1964, *11*, 324-333.

Krumboltz, J. D., Varenhorst, Barbara, B., and Thoreson, C. E. Nonverbal factors in effectiveness of models in counseling. *Journal of Counseling Psychology*, 1967, *14*, 412-418.

Leventhal, A. M. Use of a behavioral approach within a traditional psychotherapeutic context. *Journal of Abnormal Psychology*, 1968, *73*, 178-182.

Paul, G. L. *Insight versus desensitization in psychotherapy: an experiment in anxiety reduction.* Stanford, California: Stanford University Press, 1966.

Paul, G. L. Insight versus desensitization in psychotherapy two years after termination. *Journal of Consulting Psychology*, 1967, *31*, 333-348.

Robinson, F. P. *Effective Study*. (Revised Edition) New York: Harper, 1961.

Ryan, T. Antoinette and Krumboltz, J. D. Effect of planned reinforcement counseling on client decision-making behavior. *Journal of Counseling Psychology*, 1964, *11*, 315-323.

Sarbin, T. Ontogony recapitulates philology: the mythic nature of anxiety. *American Psychologist*, 1968, *23*, 411-418.

Truax, C. B. Some implications of behavior theory for psychotherapy. *Journal of Counseling Psychology*, 1966, *13*, 160-170.

Ullmann, L. P. and Krasner, L. Introduction. In Ullmann, L. P. and Krasner, L. (Eds.), *Case studies in behavior modification*. New York: Holt, Rinehart, and Winston, 1965.

Valins, S. and Ray, Alice, A. Effects of cognitive desensitization on avoidance behavior. *Journal of Personality and Social Psychology*, 1967, *7*, 345-350.

Whelan, R. J. and Haring, N. G. Modification and maintenance of behavior through systematic application of consequences. *Exceptional Children*, 1966, *32*, 281-289.

PART 2

The next section of this book presents cases similar to those a counselor working with young adults can expect to encounter. The cases are described in a manner that approximates the way counselors typically organize their observations about a client after the first, second, or third interviews. Following a discursive description of the case material, the cases are analyzed topographically and functionally in accordance with the environmental categories described in Chapter 3. From these analyses, the identification of client resources, as well as the type of problem that the client seems to be presenting, should become clearer. As a result of the understanding that grows out of the behavioral analysis, the cases are related to the counseling strategies presented in Chapter 4. Either a single strategy of preference, a hierarchy of strategies, or a sequence of strategies is described to illustrate how a counselor using the approach described in Part I of the this book works with these cases. Furthermore, sub-steps that the counselor can use to assess the degree to which he is making satisfactory progress are identified in behavioral terms.

It should be pointed out that while the cases presented are based on real people and situations, they do not each represent a single individual but are, rather, composites of cases drawn from the authors' experience. Often, these cases have been reanalyzed behaviorally to illustrate the method. This was done to preserve the privacy of the clients as well as to increase the clarity of the case presentation. It should be clearly kept in mind that these cases are not designed to *prove* that the position taken in this book is effective; nothing can be proven by case analysis. The objective of the case presentations is to show the conceptual and technical implications of an interventionistic-cognitive approach to case management in counseling. They are designed to illustrate a method.

Chapter 5

Cases

HARRY

Harry was referred to the Counseling Center during the fall quarter of his junior year. A twenty-two-year-old English major, he had recently encountered a great deal of difficulty in concentrating on his studies. He reported that every time he sat down to try to do his school work he soon became distracted by thoughts of his poor social adjustment. His social problem was causing him to earn very poor grades, to the point where the possibility of flunking out of school became a concern. Harry was living alone in a rooming house near campus and was growing increasingly aware of his isolation from other students. He was in his second year at the university, having transferred to Northern University from a smaller college after one year there. His behavior at his former college had been somewhat aggressive and hostile but no more successful socially than at Northern.

Harry was an only child of somewhat older than usual parents. The relationship between Harry and his parents was formal and minimal, particularly in recent years. Harry had grown up in a semi-rural area, separated considerably from other children and had relatively few casual friends and no really close friends. He had dated one girl for a brief period during the last year of high school, but that relationship terminated when Harry and the girl both left home to go to different colleges. Harry had little other dating and sexual experience.

Harry's behavior was characterized by constant thinking and rumination and he appeared to behave in a schizoid, obsessive-like, paranoid-like way. He kept to himself and seemed to anticipate the rejection and ridicule of other people. Often when he did interact with others he behaved aggressively, almost as if he were retaliating before these anticipated rejections. He seemed to be unable to respond to people in ways other than extreme aggressiveness on the one hand or isolative withdrawal on the other. His behavior had vacillated between these two extremes in the past; at the time Harry was seen by the counselor he was in a withdrawn state.

The situation was not entirely negative. Harry possessed a number of personal qualities that were potential assets to him. He was intelligent, interpersonally perceptive, well-read, articulate, mechanically handy, and interested in the theater and literature.

Behavioral analysis for counseling

Clarification of problem behavior. The behaviors that caused Harry difficulty in school were his isolation from others, his academic performance (apparently stemming from his ineffective studying), and the inappropriate outbursts of aggression and hostility he exhibited in his interpersonal relations at times. These behaviors appeared to have as their antecedent subjective behaviors in the form of anticipatory thoughts of rejection by other people, resentment toward them, and self-derogatory views.

Problem situation. The problem situation was very strongly associated with the scholastic environment. Obviously, if Harry left school studying would no longer be a problem. However, there was sufficient reasons to believe that much of Harry's general adjustment reflected a style of behavior that would be exhibited in nearly any context in which he would find himself. His adjustment had been characterized by his swings between aggressive and withdrawn behaviour in the past. He changed from one college to another with no serious modification of this pattern and his academic difficulties seemed to be the consequence of, and superimposed upon, his personality development, rather than the reverse. As a consequence, situational manipulation such as leaving school and getting a job did not seem to be likely to bring about a significant behavioral change.

The analysis of the educational-vocational environment. Harry's presenting concerns were in the realm of his educational achievement. Upon closer scrutiny, however, it appeared that his poor academic performance was an outcome rather than an input variable. Harry had the capability (positively reinforcing) of performing well in school. He was intelligent, articulate, well-read, and appeared to have a temperament, were he able to function normally, suitable to academic achievement. At the moment, however, the educational environment was a negative reinforcer because of his distraction over social aspects of his life and the concern he felt because of his poor current academic performance. However, it seemed likely that the academic area of Harry's life would improve were Harry able to resolve some of the personal concerns that appeared to be interfering with it.

The analysis of the family environment. Harry's family environment provided little in the way of positive or negative reinforcers. Harry maintained a considerable distance from his parents, both physically and emotionally. His parents, being considerably older than one might expect parents of a college age student to be, had maintained a diffident sort of relationship with Harry over the years. He has derived little emotional support from his parents and has grown increasingly distant and detached from them psychologically.

The analysis of the interpersonal environment. This environment appeared to be the most crucial for Harry. Many of Harry's problem behaviors were triggered by aversive types of stimuli associated with the social-sexual environment. Harry's self-derogatory thoughts centered around his anticipation of social rejection. His problem behavior of interpersonal isolation seemed to be a consequence of his lack of confidence and his expectation of social rejection. It seemed reasonable to infer that his aggressiveness at times was associated with the subjective responses relating to the anticipation of social and sexual rejection. Objectively, Harry had a number of personal attributes which offered the potential of considerable effectiveness. He was not unattractive, he was capable of being personable, and he was an interesting person in the sense of having accumulated a history of unusual and novel experiences. In addition, he had a number of socially useful talents and was knowledgeable about a number of areas which aid social popularity.

The analysis of the biological and physical attributes. Harry's health and general physical adjustment seemed normal. His recreational responses were minimal and mostly solitary, centering around listening to music and reading. However, Harry had the potential for a number of recreational responses that would contribute to his social effectiveness, notably a series of theatrically related interests and talents, such as stage crafts and stage direction.

Counseling goals and strategy

Harry's problems were treated with a behavior modification strategy aimed mainly at improving old but ineffective behaviors by encouraging Harry to use his assets in new ways. The approach to Harry's problem is best understood by identifying a series of very specific behavioral goals. It was possible to specify several classes of behavioral goals for Harry. First, and most remote in time, was the objective of making it possible for Harry to concentrate better on his work. A second set of objectives concerned reducing the frequency and intensity of Harry's self-derogatory and paranoid-like thoughts.

These thoughts, connected to Harry's tendency to alternate between isolation and aggression in his social relationships, were important to modify if Harry's ultimate well being was to improve. These classes of behaviors can be seen as a chain, which probably can be best disrupted by breaking the cycle of aggression-isolation-aggression in Harry's behavior.

To those ends, the strategy put into action with Harry ignored the performance aspects of his problems and focused, instead, on Harry's social skills. The first phase of the case was devoted to developing enough rapport between the counselor and Harry to enable the client to recognize conceptually that many of his social responses were contributing to his rejection and anticipatory thoughts of rejection and thus reduce his isolation. Harry's behavior was canvassed to discover existing behaviors that offered some potential for effective interaction with other people. The most feasible one discovered was in the realm of Harry's theatrical skills. With encouragement from the counselor, Harry entered into active work as a stagehand in theatrical groups on the campus. The theater group accepted Harry's social inadequacies simply because theatrical people are often more tolerant of socially deviant behaviors than other groups. Furthermore, the theatrical group appreciated and valued Harry's many technical skills, and communicated this appreciation to him both directly and indirectly, giving Harry a sense of self-worth. Harry, recognizing their acceptance and respect, became less defensive interpersonally. During this period of time, regular consultations were held with the counselor to discuss Harry's experiences, the counselor helping Harry polish his social insights. Because of the great impact of social reinforcement, Harry's social skills and confidence grew considerably, to the point where he began dating and feeling comfortable with a wide circle of associates. Finally, Harry began dating one girl regularly. Harry's ruminations about his inadequacy disappeared almost entirely. He found that during those periods when he needed to study he possessed a greater capability to think about his work and direct his concentration; he was no longer distracted by thoughts centered on his unsatisfied social strivings.

Harry's situation illustrates the fact that an emphasis on the positive attributes of a client can have great potential for the modification of private subjective responses which may be interfering with another realm of behavior. The approach used with Harry is in contrast to an approach emphasizing only the cognitive-performance aspects suggested by Harry's initial complaint. It is interesting to speculate upon the difference in outcome that might have occurred between the strategy used in working with Harry and one emphasizing instead the development of a work schedule and specific study skills. It might be guessed that Harry would have quickly become dissatisfied with that kind of approach and discontinued counseling, perhaps somewhat the worse since his undesirable counseling experience might have delayed the initiation of any future attempts to gain help.

CARL

This case concerns a young man, Carl D., in his early twenties, who was referred to the counselor, working in a community mental hygiene clinic, by the family physician. The client had exhibited a prolonged depression of a moderate nature. The depression appears to have been triggered by a severe auto accident suffered 6 weeks earlier in which his wife was killed. Since then, the client's depression, normal to begin with, seemed to be growing more severe. He had grown increasingly disinterested in his work and social activities, unconcerned about such things as his appearance, his diet, and the maintenance of his everyday affairs. Furhermore, he was not showing signs of terminating these deteriorative behaviors. Prior to the accident Carl had a good vocational and marital adjustment. He and his wife, married about two years, appeared to get along well. Carl was an effective salesman whose income was more than $10,000 a year and rising steadily, and who possessed a great many interpersonal skills. The couple was relatively new to the community, having moved there after their marriage when the young man obtained employment in the area.

The client, driving the car at the time of the accident, ran off the road. He suffered only very minor, superficial injuries while his wife was thrown out of the car and killed. Carl seemed to be preoccupied with blaming himself for his wife's death and appeared to be caught between his sense of relief over his survival and his feeling of guilt over that relief, since his wife did not survive. He had received a good deal of emotional support, and in fact, even more material support, from his friends and work associates, who tried to help him by distraction through invitations to their houses and by doing some of his work. Despite their efforts, he showed no signs of interest in their attempts, often failing to meet appointments or keep commitments that he made. Increasingly, he arrived at work later in the day; some days he didn't get to his office until nearly noon, and then left in mid-afternoon. When not at work, most of his time was spent simply sitting in his apartment, vacantly watching TV or just sitting and staring into space, thinking. He went to his physician at the physician's request for a checkup after his release from the hospital. Carl's behavior during the checkup concerned the physician, who observed that Carl's depression was not dissipating as it should. While some normal depression could be expected following a fatal accident, Carl's emotional recovery was not progressing satisfactorily. The physician prescribed medication to alleviate the depression but also felt that some psychological attention and supervision was necessary.

Carl's family, as well as his wife's, lived in a community about one hundred miles away. Neither family appeared to blame Carl for the unfortunate turn of events, though naturally they were extremely distressed themselves. No family members lived close enough to really provide any substantial psychological support for Carl.

Before the accident, Carl had very positive feelings about his work, his effectiveness in its performance, and its importance. During his post-accident depression, however, he began to raise questions about the worth and significance of sales work.

Such was the state of counselor knowledge at the end of a one-hour interview with Carl. On the basis of the information indicated above, a number of observations were made according to the framework of analysis presented earlier.

Behavioral analysis for counseling

Clarification of problem behavior. This part of the analysis is designed to specify the troublesome behavior, thus identifying, at least in part, the behavioral objectives to be pursued. On the basis of the preceding description, several problem behaviors were identified. These included the client's increasing tendency to isolate himself from ordinary social intercourse; his lack of attention to normal living functions such as eating, sleeping, and personal grooming; his growing failure to perform his job adequately; his failure to meet social commitments; and his state of low, general activity. These problem behaviors were probably the result of Carl's ruminations over his responsibility for the accident and his guilty feelings over surviving while his wife was mortally injured. It was reasoned that efforts to reverse or terminate Carl's depressive ruminations should first take the form of leading him to be more active physically, since physical activity would interfere with the ruminative sequences. This process could begin by getting him to talk more in the interview, which would hopefully make it possible to elicit verbal representations of Carl's poor appetite, inability to sleep, and sloppiness. Statements of intent to change would be reinforced and encouraged until better eating, sleeping and grooming behaviors, resulted. A similar sequence could be followed in connection with Carl's interaction with other people socially and on his job. Thus, a set of behavioral goals to be accomplished was established. The accomplishment of these would indicate when to terminate meeting with Carl as well as judgments about the degree of success of the outcome of the case.

Clarification of the problem situation. The clarification of the problem situation involves the analysis of the stimulus conditions and the identification of significant individuals in the environment who may be contributing to and reinforcing behavioral excesses or deficits that the client exhibits. In Carl's situation, the most prominent environmental antecedent was the automobile accident and the death of his wife. Rumination over these events reinforced the apathetic, depressive behaviors in which Carl engaged to excess. Since the ruminative behavior was disruptive and its origin can be attached to a fairly specific and concrete event, it was reasonable to expect that the intensity and frequency of the behavioral excess would decrease upon the reduction of the psychological impact of the accident either through the passage of time or by the manipulation of Carl's subjective reactions.

The analysis of the educational-work environment. This analysis is designed to describe the responses that the work environment permits the client to engage in. What reinforcing stimuli, both people and events, occur in the environment that are likely to facilitate appropriate client behavior? Similarly, what events in the environment are likely to reinforce what might be considered to be aversive responses? Furthermore, an attempt is made to identify the self-controlling elements that exist within the individual, in the institutions within which he operates, or within other individuals with whom he interacts in his educational or work environment.

In Carl's situation, a number of important reinforcers, both positive and negative in nature seemed to exist. On the positive side was the support and encouragement of Carl's work associates, his skill in the performance of his job duties before his psychological depression, his satisfaction in the performance of that work, and finally, the fact that when he was actively engaged in his work it required his full attention, thus, offering the potential of distracting him from the disruptive thoughts concerning the accident and its results. On the negative side, however, was Carl's currently poor work performance as well as his questions about the significance of the work of a salesman. An additional negative aspect of Carl's work environment was the fact that he found it difficult to interact with people following the accident, a knotty problem since interaction with people is an essential ingredient of saleswork. Finally, Carl's work required him to drive a car and driving both frightened and reminded Carl of the accident in itself, thus setting off the chain of disruptive thoughts.

The analysis of the family environment. This analysis is concerned with identification of the major influences on the client in his family, specifying the responses to the family that are likely to be acceptable to and permitted by the family members, indicating what the hierarchy is of reinforcing and aversive stimuli in that environment, and noting what, if any, self-controlling elements exist in the family environment. Carl's immediate family environment, now changed since his wife is absent, was a disruptive source of stimulation. In addition, the lack of family members in close proximity to aid Carl and provide him with continuing support to accelerate the termination of Carl's depressive reaction was unfortunate.

On the positive side, however, there was the fact that Carl and his wife were childless. The lack of children to care for simplified life for Carl, since he did not need to concern himself with such tasks as arranging for the care of youngsters while at work. It also had another positive value in that Carl remained mobile geographically and socially. Mobility enhances the ability to make a new life for oneself, a task faced by Carl. Finally, it should be noted that no overt hostile feelings from members of Carl's wife's family appeared to exist.

The analysis of the interpersonal environment. This analysis concerns itself with peer relationships, sexual relationships, and their associated deficits and excesses, as well as with the indication of what kinds of relationships with others the environment will permit. Furthermore, as in the analyses of the other environments, there is concern with the identification of the positive reinforcing and aversive hierarchies as well as the self-controlling elements in the environment. For Carl, positive factors were his youth, his sociability (before the accident) and his many friends, his sex (males possessing greater social freedom than females), and his general attractiveness and social skill.

On the negative side was the fact that women reminded him of his wife, triggering guilty thoughts and thus inhibiting his heterosexual inter-actions. In addition, there was the fact that his apartment naturally still included many possessions which reminded him of his wife and their life together; the fact that many of his friends were the mutual friends of both Carl *and* his wife was still another factor inhibiting Carl's desire to resume social contacts. Not to be ignored was the disruption of his sex life (potentially a positive factor should it motivate him to re-establish sexual-social relation-ships), and the need to become accustomed to living alone (also a potentially positive factor motivating Carl to reactivate social behaviors).

The analysis of thinking responses. This section describes the client's sub-jective responses and his self-perceptions. The description is based upon inferences drawn mainly from the client's self-report. In this connection, it was known that Carl felt guilt and responsibility for his wife's death. It is also known that Carl began questioning the meaning of his life and whether he should go on in the old style, try to create a new and different life, or just let himself deteriorate. In this regard Carl's questions about his continuing commitment to sales work were important.

The analysis of the biological and physical attributes. In this section the client's health and potential of his environment for entertainment, amusement, and diversion are assessed. Carl's environment appeared to lack suitably distracting events to interrupt the depressive ruminative thought sequences that he engaged in, which contributed to his prolonged depression. Un-fortunately for Carl there did not appear to be many significant and positive recreational features in his environment. Carl's general state of health was good, and his former psychological adjustment was satisfactory, both of which augered well for his future adjustment.

Counseling goals and strategy

On the basis of the behavioral and environmental analysis, a supportive counseling strategy seemed most appropriate to the counselor. The troublesome behavior seemed to have been elicited by a traumatic situational event. It is likely that the grief reaction following an accident such as Carl's would be expected to be severe. Superimposed on a basically sound personality, however, the reaction should begin to terminate on its own and the client should show signs of resuming his former life, or some modification of his former life. Being psychologically alone was hurting Carl's rebound. Supportive counseling can accelerate the reversal of the deteriorative process, a worthwhile goal since a prolonged grief reaction could lead to corollary problems. One way supportive counseling can help a person like Carl is to engage in a number of overt active responses to the troublesome situation. No new responses were required for Carl to improve. All that was necessary was the elicitation of former behaviors. It becomes clear from the behavioral analysis that the client possesses a wide range of socially effective responses which he was not using. To improve, it was necessary to engage Carl in those responses so that he could use his resources to terminate his reaction to what was certainly a very tragic, but not unique human situation.

A number of specific behavioral objectives were posited. The first of these was to engage the client in extended verbal interaction in the interview in order to elicit verbal representations of some of Carl's thoughts. The content of the talk was not as crucial as the fact that Carl should be encouraged to talk, although the chances were judged to be great that once Carl began to talk, the verbalization would be affective in nature and would probably deal with the accident and Carl's subjective reactions to it. Following successful elicitation of client verbalization, the counselor attempted to elicit a verbal commitment from Carl indicating that he would try to come to grips with his tragedy. This commitment then led to engaging Carl in several simple and specific behaviors that represented the first steps toward the resumption of a normal and satisfactory life. These behaviors were attending to his grooming by shaving regularly and by brushing his teeth, by awakening on a regular schedule, and, in effect, doing many of the things that he had formerly taken as a matter of course. These simple behaviors then led to more elaborate behaviors indicating movement in the direction of higher level adjustment, such as getting to work on time, beginning to associate with friends, and, in general, picking up the threads of a normal life. The efforts with Carl were thus mainly cognitive. The counselor used a supportive manner to reinforce Carl's engagement in the desired behaviors. The rationale was that for Carl, better overt behaviors would contribute to more desirable subjective behaviors.

At this point, the counselor and Carl discussed the possibility that some features of Carl's former style of life be changed. Carl concluded that he would feel more comfortable in the long run if he made a major change in his life style, but felt that the decision should not be impulsive and decided to put off a major change for at least 6 months. Carl and his counselor discussed arrangements for further counseling concerning decision-making to be held later.

To accomplish all this, the counselor first adopted the role of the concerned, understanding, and sympathetic listener. Along with these behaviors, however, the counselor gently suggested Carl engage in old and formerly effective behaviors. The counselor also verbally reinforced verbal behaviors Carl exhibited indicating reduced apathy and depressive rumination and positive commitment. As these became more numerous, the counselor encouraged Carl to engage in constructive behaviors outside of the interview. The behavioral and environmental analysis in this type of case is useful in leading the counselor to commit himself to certain minimal objectives which may be concretely and behaviorally specified. The result of the specification is the reduction of the likelihood the client will become excessively dependent on the counselor; a second result is the reduced likelihood that the client's situation will be seen to be more serious psychologically than it is. This does not deny the possibility that the client could engage in other objectives if he should choose to, but it makes those new case objectives clear and vivid to both the client and the counselor.

It is hard to see how Carl's problem could have effectively been approached from a facilitative-affective stance. Such an approach would have reinforced Carl's self-defeating behaviors. At the crucial moment in Carl's life, he needed some outside force to set his effective resources to work again.

ANN

Ann K., a college junior, was referred to the University Counseling Center in the fall quarter of the year. The referral came about after several conferences between Ann and her faculty adviser. Ann had been studying Secondary Education and was growing increasingly apprehensive about the student teaching requirement that she was tentatively scheduled to fulfill during the spring quarter of the current academic year. Ann had always been somewhat apprehensive about this aspect of her training, but recently began to appear anxious in a very general manner; she described considerable fear in connection with going off campus to fulfill the student teaching requirement. She did not specify any particular reasons for these fears to her adviser, who finally decided that Ann should consult a professional counselor before any further decisions were made concerning her student teaching placement.

In the first interview with the counselor, Ann indicated that during the previous two or three months her general (and apparently fairly normal) level of apprehension about student teaching had grown very intense and was accompanied by many of the physical manifestations of anxiety such as excessively sweaty hands, frequent periods of stomach flutters, the sensation of a dry tongue and throat, a feeling of tightness in her chest, a loss of appetite, and considerable difficulty in falling asleep at night. These manifestations of anxiety not only became more frequent, but their intensity increased considerably as well, to the point where they began to seriously disrupt her adjustment in some of her daily activities, including her academic achievement.

In searching for important connections between the feelings of anxiety that Ann was experiencing and student teaching, the counselor explored with Ann may aspects of her life outside of school. Ann described her general background in the following terms. Both her parents were teachers and Ann grew up in an atmosphere in which teaching was a major preoccupation. There were no other children in the family. Ann's parents had, as a consequence, been very attentive to her and had exposed her to many enriching experiences. At the same time, because of the close association between Ann and her parents, she had been overprotected by them. For example, Ann was a commuting student living at home. She had never been away from home on her own, that is, managing her own affairs for any extended period of time. Though he had been away from home occasionally in summers to visit relatives or to attend a camp for several weeks, she never had to set up and manage the prolonged, day-to-day affairs of a person living on her own, away from immediate family and old friends. In addition, Ann had never really seriously examined her desire to be a teacher, since both she and her parents more or less assumed that she would follow their careers. As she got further into her university program she discovered that her interests were broader than she realized. While she did not encounter any experience turning her against the possibility of teaching as a career, she did encounter a number of academic experiences which stimulated her and which could potentially lead to satisfying career possibilities other than teaching. Another notable aspect of the situation was the fact that during the spring quarter of her sophomore year, Ann became seriously attached to a young man, a student at the same university, who was to graduate the following June. His plans after graduation were unsettled, partly because of his uncertainties about being drafted, and partly because of his uncertainties about whether to attend professional school or not. It was evident, however, that some separation, at least of a temporary nature, would occur between the two of them once he graduated in June. Ann was dismayed at the prospect of moving that separation date up to the spring as a consequence of her going away to student teach.

Ann had always been a good student, who enjoyed the academic environment. She had consistently performed more than adequately in school and derived a considerable degree of satisfaction from that performance. However, she had always experienced more than the usual degree of anxiety in appearing before groups of people as a performer or as a speaker. Her anticipation of the need to speak before groups, an integral feature of teaching, added to her anxieties about the student teaching situation.

The problem, as Ann presented it to her psychologist, was clear. She realized that her anxiety was associated with the need either to accept student teaching and its consequences, or to refuse to student teach and thus be required to develop a new educational plan at a late stage of her college career. Undesirable consequences of the former decision would be separation from her boyfriend, anxiety about being on her own, and discomfort introduced by fear of the teaching situation itself. A serious consequence of the latter alternative would be the sense of letdown she thought her parents would experience were she to change her career plan, as well as the serious loss of time to graduation. She did not think her parents fully appreciated the degree of commitment she had to her boyfriend and the seriousness of their relationship, and she feared that they would not approve if they did understand. Furthermore, she had some sense of guilt over the degree of sexual intimacy (heavy petting) that had passed between her and her young man.

The information described above was obtained in the course of two fifty-minute interviews with Ann. During that time, she was taking medication prescribed by a physician to alleviate the acute aspects of her agitation. The medication was helpful, permitting Ann to resume her academic work with some effectiveness and allowing her to talk coherently with the counselor about her concerns.

Behavioral analysis for counseling

Clarification of the problem behavior. The problem behaviors in Ann's case were the physical manifestations of her anxiety, evident in a number of specific ways, e.g., sweating and stomach flutters, dry tongue and throat, tightness in chest, loss of appetite, difficulty in falling asleep, all of which occurred at very frequent intervals and to a high degree of intensity. The intensity level may be inferred from Ann's description of the difficulty she had in concentrating on her studies and maintaining a normal and productive routine. On the basis of the anxiety, it was possible to infer that there were subjective problem behaviors associated with Ann's inability to resolve the dilemma she found herself in, which she perceived to be between choosing a new program of study and thus disappointing her parents, or following through on student teaching and thus experiencing anxiety and frustration.

Analysis of the problem situation. For Ann, the problem situation had several components. The first had to do with the teaching situation itself and her fears of presenting in class, as well as fears connected with being supervised. The second was an offshoot of student teaching, that is, the need to leave home, find a place to live, and generally manage her own life without direct support from any other individual, a task which she had never done before and which she was not certain she could manage. The third component of the problem situation was also an offshoot of student teaching, i.e., the physical separation between Ann and her boyfriend. Still another aspect of the problem situation, uncertain in nature, was Ann's fear of confronting her parents with an abrupt change in plans she thought would disappoint them and lower her status in their eyes.

Analysis of the educational work environment. In this section, the client's strengths and weaknesses in his work are highlighted and the hierarchy of reinforcing and aversive conditions can be established. Ann appears to have many of the qualities necessary for success in teaching. Her verbal facility and the reinforcing value of teacher and parental approval worked toward supporting a decision to student teach; further positive reinforcers were her anticipation of potential approval from her students (if she did a good job), and the fact that she enjoyed and derived considerable satisfaction from good academic performance herself. Working against student teaching was the fact that it required her to travel away from home, meet new people, and possibly experience a critical evaluation by her supervising teacher, as well as the possibility of being unable to control the class adequately.

Analysis of family environment on her life. For Ann, the family environment consisted only of her parents. Since both were teachers they provided a positive reinforcing set of conditions for going into student teaching. The over-protective behavior of Ann's parents at an earlier time, however, had led to a series of behavioral deficits on Ann's part, specifically a lack of adequate responses to allow her to cope effectively with "independence" tasks.

The analysis of the interpersonal environment. A strongly positive reinforcer in the social-sexual realm was the fact that Ann's boyfriend was available to provide considerable emotional support in her current environment; his reinforcing value had a negative side, however, since Ann's anticipation of their eventual separation heightened her dependence on him and contributed to her difficulty in tolerating a separation from him prior to June. Additional positive aspects were Ann's personal characteristics. Her sociability and personability contributed to her ability to make friends relatively easily, even though she had a modest view of her ability to do so.

Analysis of the client's thinking behaviors. Of most value in connection with Ann's thought processes was the hierarchy of anxiety that could possibly develop in connection with certain events in Ann's life. A socially related continuum of anxiety was manufactured indicating the following: Ann could converse with one or two friends with no anxiety; speaking as a member of a class raised slight anxiety; next, and somewhat more anxiety provoking, was giving a talk at a club meeting; performing musically before an audience elicited considerable anxiety in Ann; very anxiety provoking was the need to plan and take a trip by herself; anchoring the anxious end of the continuum was the thought of starting a new job, entering a new school, or moving to a new community alone. The hierarchy of anxiety-provoking situations just described, offered potential usefulness for the conduct of desensitization trials aimed at reducing the disruptive anxiety based responses some of her thoughts stimulated.

Analysis of the biological and physical attributes. No particularly distinctive biological features appeared to be significant. It should be noted that Ann was taking medication to relieve her anxiety. Ann possessed a substantial number of recreational interests which contributed to her potential ability to make a successful adjustment to new environments and to meet new people; she was good at sports, had musical talents, danced well, and had some experience in club work and organizational work of various types.

Counseling goals and strategies

Two sets of objectives appeared reasonable for Ann. The first set, behavioral objectives, emphasized the reduction of Ann's anxiety responses. These included her difficulty in eating, sleeping, and studying, as well as the various physical distresses she experienced associated with her anxiety. The second set of objectives, more subjective in nature and antecedent to the resolution of the behavioral objectives, had to do with the dilemma that she faced in needing to choose whether to student teach or not. For that purpose, it became necessary to identify the varying strength of the antecedents of these subjective difficulties. From the analysis just completed it seemed likely that the most troublesome antecedent had to do with Ann's need to leave home in order to complete the student teaching requirement versus the need to draw up a new plan of academic action and disappoint her parents if she did not student teach.

To accomplish these objectives, a variety of strategies might have been employed, singly or in combination. Normally when support is to be used in a case, it is the first strategy to be used. In Ann's situation, where support seemed to be a necessary adjunct, it seemed reasonable to take exception to the norm and use support later in the sequence. The sequence of case management chosen was as follows: The first step was related to the need to deal directly with the anxiety responses that Ann experienced. The anxiety hierarchy discussed earlier (in the analysis of thinking behaviors) was used in a series of desensitization interviews held to reduce the anxiety Ann associated with going away from home and teaching to a sufficient degree to enable her to consider student teaching on its own merits, without anxiety (a behavior modification strategy). Following desensitization of anxiety, Ann decided she would continue with her plan to student teach, but asked for help in following the plan through. Help was provided in two respects. Extended discussion was held with Ann about how to arrange for a place to live in the community where she would student teach, along with the discussion of other practical living matters such as transportation, food shopping, etc. This segment of the case might be considered to represent a behavioral acquisition strategy.

Supportive help was provided in two ways. First, by arranging for the availability of a counselor in the new community to talk with Ann at her request and provide practical aid if she needed it. Secondly, a conference was held with Ann's boyfriend, with Ann's permission, in which he was urged to make frequent weekend visits to Ann during her student teaching quarter. Ann's anxiety level returned to a more normal state. She eventually decided (after about three months of the counseling program) to follow through with student teaching, and, though experiencing some difficulty at first, found it possible to make her own way in the new community. She did take advantage of two interviews with her "temporary" counselor while away.

By identifying the critical environmental and behavioral elements contributing to Ann's anxiety it was possible to take direct steps to reduce the anxiety enough to allow her to acquire some new behaviors which further improved her ability to cope with environmental demands. The approach used is markedly different from an approach which concentrates on client subjective feeling states paying little attention to environmental and interpersonal demands on the client.

BOB

Bob, a seventeen-year-old freshman at Eastern University, consulted a counselor at the University Counseling Center early in the fall quarter. Bob was very worried about his scholastic performance and behavior. He found himself cutting many classes, dozing as he tried to study both in the evenings and during the day. He found he was sleeping from twelve to fourteen hours a day, feeling lethargic, and without pep or enthusiasm. Bob could not account for his behavior to his satisfaction, but interpreted it as representing some unconscious resistance to the academic environment.

In high school Bob had accumulated a better than average academic record. He had never experienced any serious social-interpersonal problems, and said he had liked school. His parents were moderately well off financially and satisfied with his choice of college and academic objective. Bob was enrolled in a prelaw program, a fairly general curriculum at Eastern University allowing a varied number of educational opportunities to unfold over the years. Bob said he felt no discomfort about the tentativeness of his academic commitment and said he felt that more structure would occur with respect to his academic objectives as he progressed through the university. At that time Bob's older brother was in college (not Eastern University) and his younger sister was in the 10th grade. Bob reported that he and his brother and sister were close to one another and got along well together.

Upon retrospect in the interview with the counselor, Bob noted that he became easily tired while in high school, but never to the degree he was experiencing since his arrival at Eastern. There had been a marked increase in his fatigue over the summer, which Bob attributed to his anticipatory fears about coming to the university.

Behavioral analysis for counseling

Clarification of the problem behavior. Problem behaviors may be specified for Bob; these were primarily sleeping inappropriately (at the wrong time) and sleeping excessively. When awake, Bob functioned effectively.

Clarification of the problem situation. No particular situational elements in the academic environment seemed likely to be associated with the troublesome sleeping behavior. It was notable that the sleeping behaviors were not present to a disruptive degree when Bob was at home in high school.

Analysis of the educational-work environment. Examination of Bob's previous educational adjustment indicated that Bob possessed the appropriate responses for success in an educational environment and further, that he found the educational environment possessed many positively reinforcing objects, people, and events. In the past, he had exhibited sufficient self-controlling behaviors to function effectively academically.

Analysis of the family environment. Bob reported family relationships which seemed satisfactory and relatively normal. His relationship with his parents seemed appropriate but not excessively close and essentially supportive in nature. His sibling relationships also appeared to be close and supportive, but not dependent.

The analysis of the interpersonal environment. Bob appeared to have experienced success in his social relationships in the past indicating that he possessed adequate response capabilities to function effectively socially in college.

In the past, the social environment had been a positive, reinforcing environment to Bob. In his current situation, however, Bob's sleepiness was interfering with his social success.

Analysis of the thinking process. Bob was unable to report any substantial psychological event or events that might have contributed to his growing lethargy. Bob assumed there were some unconscious motives involved that led him to try to avoid something in his new environment, but he had no clue as to what events or motives might be involved.

Analysis of the biological and physical attributes. Bob appeared to be in good health; his environment and his response capabilities seemed to indicate the availability of appropriate recreational responses. However, the counselor became concerned about the potential physical implications of what appeared to be a rather abrupt change in Bob's energy level, and consequently, suggested to Bob that he consult the University Health Center for a physical examination in connection with these behaviors as a precaution. The results of the physical examination indicated that Bob had a significantly underactive thyroid gland. The physician recommended medical treatment for the condition. The examining physician did not feel it was out of the question for Bob's lethargy to have been associated with his social and academic ineffectiveness.

Counseling goals and strategy

Bob's case was continued under the supervision of the counselor for several weeks following the beginning of medical treatment for the underactive thyroid condition. It soon became evident that Bob's physical lethargy and inability to attend classes and concentrate on his studies as well as his inability to adjust satisfactorily socially was probably the result of his thyroid condition. He became more energetic and his sleeping behavior returned to normal. He was sleeping eight or nine hours a day, did not have excessive difficulty staying awake in class or reading and studying, and found that he became more energetic about pursuing his social activities. After several weeks of such supervision both the counselor and Bob were convinced that there wasn't any subconscious motivational problem involved, but rather a clear-cut physical deficiency, and the case was terminated.

This case illustrates in a dramatic fashion several interesting problems that counselors can encounter. Were the counselor not trying to get thorough information about each of the environmental areas, he might have overlooked the possibility of a physical cause for Bob's behavior. Verbal methods in such a case would obviously have been totally ineffective, and Bob's physical condition, as well as his academic and social condition, would have

continued to deteriorate, probably to the point where Bob would have had
to leave school, somewhat bewildered about his failure. Because Bob was
prepared to think of his behavior in psychological terms as many people
are prone to do, the counselor almost overlooked the possibility that a
physical cause was involved. Routine as it may be, and irrelevant as it may
often turn out to be, it is good for the counselor to remind himself that
sometimes physical antecedents to behavior problems exist which can be
easily and directly corrected if proper steps are taken to diagnose the
condition.

ED

Ed came to State University as a freshman in mid-September, full of
misgivings about his first term living away from home and family and about
his chances for success at the Univesity. Ed had been neither a distinguished
scholar nor a school leader at home. In fact, he would have been content to
stay home and get a job, were it not for the fact that all his friends went to
college and it was expected that anybody who had the opportunity to do so
would attend. By the end of the first week of classes Ed began to grow
listless and apathetic; he took to missing meals, staying by himself, cutting
class, and remaining in his room for most of the day; he was sleeping as
much as ten to twelve hours every day. By the end of the second week of class,
Ed's residence hall counselor began to notice Ed's withdrawn behavior
and grew concerned. He tried on two occasions to draw Ed out and talk
with him about the troublesome behavior. The most he was able to elicit
was a statement from Ed that he thought he was homesick and that he was
thinking of leaving school and returning home. Among the list of complaints
that Ed mentioned were his distaste for the food in the dormitory, his
missing his old friends and inability to make new friends, his concern about
his performance in course work, and the nature of school work in general.
In addition, he found his roommate to be objectionable, was concerned
that he was wasting his family's money by being in school, missed having a
car to drive, and yearned for his old part-time job. After two conversations,
the residence hall counselor suggested that before Ed did anything precipitate,
he talk with a counselor at the University Counseling Center. This suggestion
seemed reasonable to Ed, particularly since he thought that a counselor
would reinforce his resolve to leave the university.

He made arrangements to see one of the university counselors promptly.
There he repeated a similar story, adding several facts which made Ed's
situation even more understandable. These were, first, the fact that he was
not scholastically oriented in high school. That is to say, Ed neither found
scholastic tasks particularly gratifying nor did he excel in them. Furthermore,

he never felt particularly pleased on those few occasions when he did a reasonably good job in some school task. His interests did not run to reading or reflecting over events and analyzing the relationships between symbols. Ed further reported the fact that he had no particular educational objective. He was enrolled in engineering and had been overwhelmed by the demands of the courses very quickly. His background in mathematics and science was not strong and his interest even weaker. He chose engineering simply because it seemed like a concrete, practical discipline which offered the possibility of earning a good living. It appealed to his sense of masculinity but it did not present him with a series of tasks that he found interesting and competent to perform. Third, Ed was experiencing a sense of isolation at the university. He felt alone, separated from others, afraid that he would fail in school and afraid that he would be rejected by his peers if he were to make overtures of friendship to them. Ed further elaborated on his creature complaints, such as the poor food and lack of money and car, but it became clear that these latter complaints were less significant to Ed than the former ones. It seemed likely that if Ed were able to function more effectively scholastically and perform better in a more cogent academic objective than engineering, and if he were able to overcome his sense of isolation and make suitable social contacts, these latter complaints would assume their proper proportion in his mind.

Behavioral analysis for counseling

The analysis of the problem behaviors. Of the number of problem behaviors that could be identified, the most cogent ones seemed to be the absence of certain important coping responses such as study skills, decision-making, and social responses that would result in making new friends. In addition, other behaviors existed that interfered with the development of adequate coping behaviors; these interfering behaviors were self-isolation, lethargy (exhibited in excessive sleeping), and cutting classes.

The analysis of the problem situation. Ed's situation presented the curious phenomenon of an individual who was able to cope adequately and get along reasonably well in one environment, but, when lifted out of that environment and placed in a new context, could not exhibit the responses needed to cope effectively with the demands of the new situation. While there were no data to indicate very clearly how he would function in a wide range of situations, it did appear clear that Ed's current difficulty seemed closely tied to his current scholastic environment. For example, if Ed left school and were able to go home, it seemed very likely that his lethargy, his sense of isolation, and what appeared to be a mild depression would disappear and he would function better. This suggested then, that one kind of treatment to be considered was a direct situational manipulation; a drastic solution, however, and one appropriately reserved for use after less drastic methods have been tried and shown to be ineffective.

The analysis of the educational-vocational environment. This segment of the behavioral analysis possessed considerable saliency for Ed. The educational environment that he found himself in presented a great many tasks that were either difficult for Ed to perform, uninteresting to him, or both. Part of the difficulty appeared to be Ed's deficient study skills and lack of other behaviors that would enhance his academic performance. Another feature had to do with the question about the appropriateness of Ed's temperament and aptitudes for high level abstract academic tasks. Apparently, Ed had never seriously contemplated vocational choice and commitment, and had, instead, drifted along with the implicit expectation that events themselves would determine his future occupational activity satisfactorily. In fact, Ed did not appear to have strong likes or dislikes about work activities, though it did appear that on the basis of his previous performance, his interests were not scholarly, but instead required physical action and activity in order to be satisfied. His scholastic performance in the past, as well as his scores on academic aptitude tests, indicated that he possessed the minimum intellectual attributes to complete a university education, but hardly in a curriculum as demanding as engineering. At the point of beginning college, the educational environment possessed a great many aversive stimuli to Ed and virtually no reinforcers. Were certain aspects of this environment modified, that is, were he to find that he could perform more effectively without an inordinate amount of added work, and were he to find that some of his work tasks were not unpleasant, and perhaps even provided a modicum of internal subjective gratification, the academic situation might develop into at least a mildly reinforcing environment. For Ed, however, in view of the problem behaviors occurring in school, the educational and vocational environment appeared to be one of critical importance.

The analysis of the family environment. Ed's family was large. He had four older sisters and one younger brother. His father was an engineer; his mother went to college, but did not graduate. Ed, being the older son, felt considerable pressure to earn a college degree and enhance the family name. Actually, however, he reported getting little support either financially or psychologically from his parents toward completing the degree. His relations with his parents were detached and distant; he was closer emotionally and got more support from his older sisters, whom he missed considerably. His home was in a medium-size community about two hours drive from school. Among the family supports that he missed was the frequent use of the family car, the fact that one of his brothers-in-law allowed him to use his car almost at will, and the fact that he had a very enjoyable part-time job working for another brother-in-law in his retail business. The family situation had thus provided a great many positive supports to maintain his adjustment while he remained at home. As a consequence, leaving home and separating himself from those supports added to the aversiveness associated with enrolling in college. At the same time, quitting school and going home would be embarrassing and distressing to him, since he feared the reaction his family would have would be derogatory and critical.

Interpersonal relations. Ed did not date at all. He wanted to, but lacked skill in meeting and talking to girls. He had little social experience and doubted his ability to function effectively on a date. These self-perceptions were another facet of his self-criticism. They also kept him isolated from certain kinds of college activities which are basically heterosexual in nature. Furthermore, his social timidity interfered with his ability to make male friends, as well as female ones, since many young men he might have been associating with were very active socially and dating extensively. To add to his difficulties, his roommate was a slick, sophisticated well-to-do, urban girl chaser who mocked Ed's social reticence. Thus, the social-sexual realm for Ed provided a great many aversive stimuli and, while potentially might be a potent reinforcer to remain in school, was, in fact, a very potent force stimulating him to consider leaving the university.

The analysis of thinking responses. Ed's thoughts centered about himself and his current adjustment in school. He was very self-critical and engaged in a great many self-derogatory thoughts. He anticipated failure, was concerned over his lack of academic motivation, skill and commitment, and at times, thought it would be easier to return home and go to work for his brother-in-law rather than persist through four years of the distress he was then experiencing. Such thoughts had preoccupied him since a few weeks before he began his university career.

Biological and physical attributes. No special biological characteristics about Ed were notable. The recreational environment in college for Ed was primarily an aversive stimulus largely as a result of Ed's outdoor orientation and the fact that going to college took time away from his opportunities to be outside hunting, fishing, and engaging in sports. Thus, the area of recreational possibilities added still another stimulus source driving Ed away from the university.

Counseling goals and strategy

A major question involved in Ed's situation was whether or not his desire to leave the university was primarily a complex of avoidance behaviors in response to a set of aversive conditions experienced in school or whether it was primarily the result of a set of approach responses to another stimulus environment (home). The behavioral and environmental analysis suggested that Ed's desire to leave the university stemmed more from his desire to avoid a set of aversive consequences in the educational, social, and re-creational environments associated with the university, than a desire to return to a comfortable environment, although home had some "approach" features connected with it. As a consequence, strategies employed with Ed emphasized operations that reduced the potency and frequency of the aversive stimuli in school and thus enabled him to function more effectively in his current environment. The rationale was that as school became more attractive to him, home would by contrast, have a weaker pull.

A sequence of strategies seemed to be in order. The first of these was to work on the question of Ed's academic performance, one of the prepotent aversive conditions. Here, a strategy of performance improvement seemed to be in order. The approach entailed close analysis and supervision of Ed's work habits and functioning.

At the same time, a behavior acquisition strategy to improve Ed's social skills was also applied. Ed did not experience much anxiety in anticipating social interaction, but he did need to learn certain social behaviors that would enable him to function more effectively with other people, par-ticularly girls. Improved interpersonal feedback was expected to lead to the extinction of his sense of inadequacy and lack of self-confidence. Thus, it was thought Ed's interpersonal effectiveness should improve rapidly once the treatment effects were set in motion, since the new behaviors would themselves be reinforced and reinforcing, and would at the same time con-tribute to the extinction of the old, ineffective behaviors, thus producing a double-barrelled effect.

Of prime importance was Ed's need to make some immediate decisions about his academic major. It seemed clear that Ed should not be in engin-eering, but instead should be in some general program which would give him an opportunity to explore his interests and talents, and offer the possibility of finding something satisfying in the academic world. Promising directions to explore included programs which would allow him to express his outdoor interests, and interpersonal skills, one such as conservation, biological science, agriculture, physical education, or recreation education.

To these ends then, the first step taken was to enlist Ed's agreement that it was reasonable to explore certain avenues associated with better adjustment before leaving the university. Following Ed's agreement, an interest inventory and a scholastic aptitude test were administered to him. On the basis of those results, it was eventually decided that Ed would change his program from engineering to agriculture where he would major in agricultural business. This move enabled him to employ his retailing interests in a context which allowed the expression of his outdoor interests. The prospect of curricular change alone had a major impact on Ed's academic behavior and performance, because he felt optimistic about his interest and achievement in his new academic situation.

Though the change in program could not be implemented until the end of the quarter, Ed promptly felt his presence at the university had more significance for his later life. As a consequence, Ed became more receptive than before to suggestions about organizing his academic affairs and working more efficiently. The counselor showed Ed several techniques for effective studying, all of which emphasized the overt manifestation of studying behavior, i.e., note-taking, outlining, self-quizzes, and recitation. The effect of these was to make the study task external, bringing it under more direct cognitive control, and making lapses in concentration and effectiveness evident quickly. The counselor's role during this phase was that of encouraging coach.

After about two months of concentrating on his educational and vocational adjustment, during which time the counselor served largely as an academic coach, the counseling changed its focus to the social-sexual realm of Ed's life. Ed was beginning to perceive increasing discomfort socially, largely because of the growing contrast between his educational-vocational adjustment and his social failures. In this connection, some discussion was initiated by the counselor centering on Ed's feelings and concern about his physical appearance, his dress, and his lack of social graces. Ed was embarrassed by his unstylish dress, and judged himself to be unusually homely, though he was in fact not exceptional one way or another in his appearance. Steps were taken to help Ed learn how he might be expected to behave socially in new situations and he began to function with some increased effectiveness. Questions of dress, manners, introductions, and engaging in simple social conversation were discussed. Ed's total expectations were thus manipulated cognitively. After three such interviews, though Ed still had some anxiety about approaching a girl for a date, he began to practice his social skills outside the interview room by forcing himself to talk to girls after class. Soon he was going for informal dates. Within a month, Ed was beginning to date, and though still feeling somewhat uncomfortable with girls, was optimistic about his chances to be more effective socially. Academically, his performance was acceptable and satisfying and Ed was no longer entertaining thoughts of leaving the university four months after beginning counseling.

The program of treatment followed in working with Ed was almost entirely cognitive in nature. The distinctive sequential aspects of the strategy first showed Ed how the university could become more relevant to his purpose in life. Following the increased motivation resulting from Ed's changed attitude toward school he was open to learning academic skills for the first time in his life, once again, a cognitive task. As a result of the increased effectiveness he demonstrated scholastically following the two cognitive restructurings, Ed began to develop both a sense of achievement and a desire to feed it. As his achievements grew, Ed developed an interest in furthering his social skills along with a growing confidence in his ability to do so. Thus, he was open to social skill learning, leading to improved social techniques. These experiences were primarily cognitive in nature, but led to an affective subjective change in Ed's attitude toward his social value and effectiveness. This last change encouraged Ed to expose himself to experiences which were increasingly reinforcing socially.

The tack followed was very different from others that might have been taken. If, for example, the counselor had merely followed a reflective technique, Ed's anxieties about his social and educational adequacies would very likely have been reinforced. Under increased anxiety it seems doubtful that Ed would have had any other recourse but to leave school prematurely, possibly being haunted by a sense of failure indefinitely.

Similarly, a counselor using a test-oriented approach might have successfully demonstrated Ed's shortcomings in engineering as well as his strengths for other programs, but without providing the means to integrate the information into behaviors leading to changed plans, attitudes, and techniques, Ed would have been left to flounder. Once again, the outcome would probably have led to failure and embarrassment.

Instead, the approach followed both provided Ed with some new concepts about himself, the university, and the future, and some means through which he could implement these new understandings in an environment that was once filled with threat.

BART

Bart was an eighteen-year-old male college freshman attending Southern University with no defined college major. During his first quarter at the university his academic performance was below average. Bart reported that he was confused and overwhelmed by the academic courses and that he did not know how to study. He also reported feeling depressed because of his unsatisfactory academic performance.

Bart lived at home with his mother, father, and one brother. His father was employed as a painter and earned about $6,000 a year. Bart's brother, a fourth quarter university student (no defined college major) with a history of academic problems, was currently on academic probation at Southern. In general, the boy's parents did not seem to value a college education. Bart's mother had completed high school and his father left school after tenth grade. They seemed to think that education beyond high school was a waste of time. Therefore, they exerted pressure on both Bart and his brother to leave school, find work and assume a portion of the financial responsibility at home.

During high school Bart's academic performance (above average) had been a source of satisfaction to him even though, and possibly partly because, it required a minimum of preparation. He graduated 35th in his senior class of 100. His American College Test composite score reflected above average academic potential. Bart had also enjoyed his membership on the high school basketball team. He hoped to play college basketball and his high school coach had encouraged the aspiration. In addition, Bart seemed to be socially active and well-liked in high school. Presently, Bart had a steady girl friend, Sue, age 18, whom he had been dating for two years. Sue, a home town girl, was also a second quarter freshman at the University, majoring in Home Economics, and seemed to be a well-adjusted girl with marriage on her mind.

Behavioral analysis for counseling

Clarification of problem behavior. Bart had never learned the adaptive complex of responses known as study skills (coping behavior). The behavioral deficit largely stemmed from Bart's limited academic experience. In high school the academic work was not sufficiently rigorous to require Bart to acquire and implement high level study skills. In general, Bart's study behaviors were infrequent, inappropriate in form, erratic and unrewarding.

Clarification of the problem situation. Bart, commuting between home and school, worked three hours each weekday and eight hours on Saturday in a clothing store in order to finance his education. Most of the studying he tried to do was while at home. Bart's brother, a fourth quarter sophomore on academic probation, interfered with the development of an atmosphere conducive to effective study. He often had friends in the house or otherwise bothered Bart during study hours. In addition, other aspects of Bart's home environment were not suitable for study since his parents thought college was a waste of time and often made comments to that effect. Offsetting the problems was Bart's pleasure in recalling his good academic performance in high school. At the time he sought counseling, Bart found he became anxious prior to an examination, and grew depressed when he performed below average on an examination. He reported that he did not know how to break the cycle of anxiety-poor-performance-depression. Adding to Bart's discomfort was his awareness that he had to earn satisfactory grades in order to be eligible to play basketball.

Analysis of the educational-work environment. The academic environment required the acquisition of adaptive studing behavior. Bart's response deficit in that environment had to be reduced if Bart were to function effectively in the academic environment.

In analyzing Bart's educational environment, a hierarchy of reinforcing stimuli that could improve his ability to study was identified. First was Bart's satisfaction in recalling his above average academic performance in high school. Certainly, Bart's ACT composite score suggested that he possessed the potential to respond effectively to academic demands. A second reinforcing element was the high school guidance counselor who had been a source of encouragement for Bart. The counselor had communicated his belief to Bart that he had the ability to earn a degree.

Other events encouraged Bart. His aspiration to play college basketball was also related to his desire to perform well academically. Although Bart's grades for the fall quarter were generally low, he did achieve an "A" grade in college algebra. In a recent discussion with his adviser, Bart had been encouraged to continue college and to seek help in studying. Financial aid (either through an academic scholarship or a basketball scholarship) was available to Bart if his academic performance was satisfactory. Even Bart's employer at the clothing store encouraged him to continue college, adding to Bart's sense of commitment to college.

A hierarchy of aversive stimuli associated with Bart's educational environment could also be observed. One such stimulus was Bart's low grade point average for the fall quarter, causing him to be placed on academic probation, and, as a consequence, forcing him to drop freshman basketball. A second aversive event was the advice of Bart's instructor in his college English course that Bart leave college.

Analysis of the family environment. Bart's family no only failed to support the acquisition of study behavior, but actively interfered. Pressure existed at home for him to get a job in order to assume a portion of the financial responsibility at home. In addition, his parent's devaluation of a college education and his brother's academic problems caused Bart to doubt his academic commitment at times. Since Bart was receiving no financial aid from home, his part-time job was necessary in order to maintain himself, but necessarily reduced time available for study. Though of less importance the hierarchy of positive reinforcing stimuli in the family included his brother's desire to obtain a college degree and the encouragement of his family doctor to continue college.

Interpersonal relationships. Bart's social environment permitted the acquisition of study behavior. No other behavioral excesses or deficits seemed to be troublesome in the social environment. The hierarchy of reinforcing stimuli in the social environment had three components. First, was the importance Bart's girlfriend placed on a college education. Next, were Bart's high school basketball coach and employer, who have encouraged him to persist in college. Last, was Bart's peer group who perceived a college education to be of considerable value. All of the peer group's members were attending college, and many were evidencing academic problems similar to Bart's.

The aversive hierarchy included the fact that no financial aid was currently available to Bart. Also, friends of Bart's parents reinforced their derogatory attitude toward higher education, adding to parental pressure to leave school.

Analysis of the thinking process. Bart perceived himself as being academically ineffective. This perception of ineffectiveness was beginning to generalize to other areas of his life, notably social. He was beginning to think that his academic ineffectiveness indicated a general unworthiness and inadequacy. Bart was also developing feelings of guilt because of the incongruence between his parents' attitudes about education an his own values in general.

Biological and physical attributes. A recent physical examination for freshmen basketball players' indicated that Bart was in good health and physical condition. Bart still played basketball on a regular schedule even though he was not officially a member of the freshman basketball team.

Goals and strategies

The strategy implemented in working with Bart was that of performance improvement. The goal of this strategy was the acquisition of effective study behaviors and the improvement of existing study behaviors, in accordance with Bart's objective of earning better grades. A corollary goal in this connection was to change the parental attitude about higher education.

To accomplish the goal of improved performance a modified version of the SQ3R study method was used. Bart's American History course was the target for this technique. The modified technique involved surveying the textbook, writing out questions from the topic sentences in a chapter, writing out the answers to the questions, reading, reciting, and reviewing. The behavioral value of writing was that studying then acquired a concrete referent for Bart, bringing it under his control more directly than before. Once the working notes (written questions with written answers) were prepared for a given chapter Bart then used these for review. Bart also made a list of important terms along with their definitions. Each week Bart would bring working notes to his counselor for critical review and recitation. In addition, with the counselor's aid, Bart developed a time sheet which showed how he spent his time, after which he devised a new time plan committing himself to studying four hours each day, except on weekends.

Early in the winter quarter Bart enrolled in a reading course in order to improve his reading rate and comprehension. His attention was directed to his classroom behavior, where he was given instruction in improved note taking, making his notes both more legible and meaningful upon review. In general, Bart was motivated to acquire and improve his academic skills. He seemed to be making satisfactory progress.

In order to have an effective academic environment in which to study, Bart began to work at the University Library at night. To improve his home environment Bart and the counselor decided the counselor would write a letter to Bart's parents discussing the practical and vocational value of a college education. The parents were also asked to attend a career night at the University with the hope that they would acquire some understanding of the educational process. The counselor, with Bart's consent, and the parents' invitation, visited Bart's home to respond to questions and hopefully modify, to some degree, their attitude toward higher education. The above efforts, concomitant with the counseling sessions, aided Bart to reduce the discomfort he felt about the incongruence between his parents' attitudes and his own.

After mid-term examinations during the winter quarter, Bart's academic work showed improvement. He was no longer on probation. Bart now expressed concern about his "undecided" academic status. He felt he should be working toward identifying a college major. Bart and his counselor embarked on a decision-making strategy whose goal was the selection of a college major. Bart expressed an interest in medicine but added that he had many doubts about his suitability for a medical career. Bart's inventoried interests supported his expressed interest in medicine, but he felt the need for additional information about the profession and his manifest interests as well as his abilities. Bart's plan of action was to work as an orderly in a hospital for the summer while at the same time to seek information about the pre-medical program at the University. On this note the case ended.

Summary. Bart came to the counseling center because he was overwhelmed by the academic course work at the University, and did not know how to study. Bart perceived himself to be academically inadequate. This perception of ineffectiveness was beginning to generalize to the social aspects of his life. The first strategy used in working with Bart was that of performance improvement, whose goal was the acquisition of effective study behaviors and the improvement of existing study behaviors. After a month of aid from the counselor in the role of study coach, Bart's work showed significant improvement. The counselor also helped Bart come to terms with his parents' antagonism toward higher education, which allowed Bart to feel more comfortable in the pursuit of his academic goals. The second approach implemented in working with Bart was that of decision making. The specific goal of this strategy was the selection of a college major. Using a combination of interest inventories, interviews, information, and work experience, Bart embarked on a program of educational-vocational decision making.

Working with Bart in this case, the counselor emphasized cognitive and situational variables. After assuring himself about the nature of the antecedents the counselor tried to clear the way environmentally for Bart to use his intellectual skills effectively; the counselor did not respond emphatically to the affective aspects of Bart's concerns, seeing them as outcomes of more basic cognitive inadequacies.

RAY

Ray was a nineteen-year-old, fifth quarter sophomore at Southern University majoring in Electrical Engineering when the first saw his counselor as a self-referral. Though his academic performance was adequate (about average), Ray was ambivalent about his college major and wanted to explore his abilities, vocational interests, and life goals.

Ray lived in a residence hall with two other students at Southern University. His father, a demanding, dominant, independent man was employed as a professional engineer and earned approximately $25,000 a year. His mother was very socially-oriented and had for years devoted much of her time to various community and club activities. Both parents valued higher education, particularly the practical and applied kind. Pressure had been put on Ray for a number of years to major in engineering. He had considered a career in medicine before he came to college but his parents (in particular, his father) did not care to discuss the alternative. Ray's younger brother Ed, age 18, enlisted in the Navy upon the completion of high school.

Test data suggested that Ray's inventoried interests were incongruent with his college major. The SVIB profile reflected a primary interest pattern in the business contact group and a secondary interest pattern in the social service group and the verbal-linguistic group. These data suggested that Ray's major career orientation was toward interpersonal activity rather than objects. Ray's scholastic aptitude (inferred from his ACT percentile score of 85) was compatible with his engineering major. However, his academic performance was below the potential suggested by the aptitude test results.

Ray's career choice seemed to have been influenced by his father. In fact Ray's father had made most of Ray's significant decisions. Ray was not happy with this dependency status but an offsetting consequence for him lay in the benefit of being released from the responsibility of making decisions. Usually, if Ray's father did not make a necessary decision, Ray became very anxious (manifest in insomnia, social withdrawal, procrastination, and perseveration) and he eventually permitted circumstances to force the decision. In that manner, he thus managed to be released from the responsibility of actively making a decision and he would not have to be concerned about his father's reaction to a decision that he made, since he had avoided committing himself.

Behavioral analysis for counseling

Clarification of problem behavior. Ray was dissatisfied with his college major. He expressed an interest in exploring various possible college major alternatives. The data suggested that Ray had not learned the complex adaptive responses involved in decision making. His behavioral deficit seemed to stem from the interfering effect of anxiety. He was concerned about the responses of his father if he erred. In a decision making situation, Ray's behavior was characterized by procrastination, perseveration, and withdrawal.

Clarification of the problem situation. Ray's original college major was based on parental pressure and goals. He neither overtly expressed the desire nor made the decision to major in electrical engineering. Ray was really vocationally undecided, partly because of a lack of information, but primarily because making such a decision was anxiety arousing. His perception was that making a vocational-educational decision would involve defying his parents. Therefore, the client avoided the anxiety by not making any vocational-educational decision.

Analysis of the educational or work environment. The educational environment permitted the acquisition of decision making behaviors. Thus, it was reasonable to assume that a modification of Ray's response deficit would improve his academic and social effectiveness.

In analyzing Ray's educational environment, it was possible to identify certain reinforcing stimuli that offered the potential to facilitate decision-making behaviors. One such reinforcing event was Ray's enjoyment of the educational environment; another was his satisfaction in being away from home. In addition, Ray had independently acquired a part-time job working in a clothing store, which required him to open the store three days a week. He experienced much satisfaction in connection with his responsibility. A fourth reinforcing stimulus was the fact that since Ray's academic work had been satisfactory, he felt relatively secure in an academic environment. Academically, he had the basic skills necessary to cope with the demands placed upon him. Finally, during his fourth quarter, Ray completed a course in business law (with the grade of A) and found the academic content interesting and the experience gratifying.

A hierarchy of aversive stimuli associated with Ray's academic environment was also observed. One aversive stimulus was Ray's dissatisfaction with the electrical engineering curriculum. It will be recalled that the test data suggested that Ray's major orientation was toward people rather than things. In addition, Ray's adviser, a domineering, authoritarian person who made academic decisions for Ray, reminded him of his father and elicited similar responses from Ray. As a result, the adviser further served inappropriately to remove the responsibility for academic decision-making from Ray and unwittingly undermined Ray's decision-making skills.

Analysis of the family environment. The family environment actively interfered with Ray's acquisition of decision-making behaviors. In the past, his parents had frequently made decisions for Ray. For example, Ray had not been permitted to play football in high school; he was allowed to date only on Saturday night; he was required to study Sunday through Thursday nights; and in college he was to major in engineering. Furthermore, Ray's parents made it a point to visit him ever other Sunday at Southern University. The frequency of their visits made Ray anxious particularly when he thought about making a decision that would defy his parents.

A curiously positive reinforcing stimulus was Ray's contentment with his personal life away from home, though his academic dissatisfaction offset this contentment. This suggested that he would like the opportunity to behave more independently than he had been able to in the past.

Interpersonal relationships. A positive reinforcing stimulus in Ray's social environment was the relationship he had developed with Judy. Ray met Judy during his third quarter and had been dating her since that time. She was a college sophomore majoring in liberal arts.

Ray's male peer relationships had been limited to his two roommates in the residence hall. Both of Ray's roommates tended to make decisions for him or about him. For example, Richard and Fred, individually or together made decisions about where to eat, studying hours in the room, time for lights to be out, etc. In general, they controlled the environment without consulting Ray.

Analysis of the thinking process. Ray was aware of his perservative avoidant tendencies in decision-making situations. He also ruminated extensively over his concern with defying his parents and his anxiety when confronted with the need to make a choice which his parents might dislike. At the same time, he was sufficiently realistic to understand that his anxiety and pattern of thinking was inappropriate and ineffective. He came to the counseling center to change this thought pattern and behavior. Ray wanted to be able to control his behavior and actively make decisions.

Biological and physical attributes. A pre-college physical examination indicated that Ray's physical condition was satisfactory. Ray was still taking the course in physical education required by the University of students in their first two years.

Counseling goals and strategy

The strategy implemented in working with Ray was a combination of behavior modification and decision making. The goals of this strategy were the reduction of anxiety associated with decision making, the acquisition of effective decision making behaviors, and the implementation of these behaviors.

To accomplish the goal of anxiety reduction, the counselor elicited talk from Ray about the anxiety feelings associated with defying his parents. In talking with the counselor about the anxiety provoking stimulus, Ray began to experience anxiety as he reviewed specific situations. However, since in the interview the anxiety was not reinforced, Ray's anxiety associated with thoughts of defying his parents was reduced; his anxiety was thus gradually desensitized.

The next goal involved the acquisition of new behaviors. Ray wanted to assume active control over his behavior. In the past others had made decisions for him. In many situations, he had assumed a passive role so that eventually circumstances determined the decision for him. Ray wanted to act more independently but didn't know how.

Ray perceived, and the counselor reinforced, the sub-goal in the behavior acquisition process of becoming more assertive with his roommates. Ray began to attempt to engage in the decisions about room management that Richard and Fred heretofore made. For example, the three discussed the task of cleaning the room and agreed upon times to watch TV, play records, and study. A second sub-goal introduced by the counselor involved Ray's becoming more active in structuring his academic program with his adviser. He discussed with his adviser the idea of taking some elective courses in business administration. With the encouragement of the counselor, Ray informed his adviser that he was dissatisfied with the engineering program and wanted his adviser's aid in considering various alternatives. The adviser referred Ray to a personal friend in the college of business administration for further information. A final, behavioral sub-goal for Ray was the increased frequency of engaging in independent behavior associated with his parents. For example, Ray, with the counselor's support, mentioned to his parents that he was dissatisfied with engineering and that he was considering other alternatives including that of a summer job away from home. In essence, Ray was beginning to assume the responsibility for his life and structure his own long term goals by taking action in appropriate ways. He found that some anticipated aversive consequences did not materialize.

As counseling went on, Ray wanted to reach some decision about a new college major. He had no strong educational preferences to offset his aversion to the engineering program, but he did mention the positive experience he had in the business law course and his satisfaction with the job in the retail business.

The client's dissatisfaction with engineering was further clarified by means of the counseling process and the test data. He gained the understanding that he was more likely to be satisfied working with people, and grew to realize the implications of that understanding. He began to see the possibility of satisfaction in a career in business or law. These areas of work seemed to be more consistent with Ray's interests, aptitudes, and needs than any others. Since Ray expressed a lack of information about occupations in the business area, he was referred to the occupational information library and to the College of Business Administration. In addition, Ray, with the counselor's aid, found summer employment where he was able to acquire additional experience in sales. The counselor suggested, and Ray agreed, that his current thinking and new educational-vocational plan should be discussed with his parents. Ray agreed to see the counselor again in the autumn after the summer vacation.

Ray eventually decided to transfer to a pre-law program with the expectation that upon graduation he could either attend law school or pursue an M.A. degree in Business Administration.

Summary. Ray came to the counseling center reporting that he was dissatisfied with his college major. He wanted to explore his abilities, vocational interests, and life goals. Observation suggested that Ray had not learned the complex adaptive responses involved in decision making because family based anxiety had prevented Ray from learning this behavior. The approach used in working with Ray was a combination of behavior modification and decision making. The goals of this approach involved the reduction of anxiety associated with the decision-making, the acquisition of effective decision-making behaviors and the implementation of these behaviors, along with the development of interpersonal assertive responses that enabled Ray to participate more fully in decisions that concerned him.

CAROL

Carol was a college sophomore majoring in the Arts and Letters College when she first consulted her counselor at the University Counseling Center. Carol was an attractive young woman, nineteen years old, who came from a well-to-do family who lived in an urban area about 200 miles away from the campus of Southwestern University. Carol had no strong academic or vocational goals, but generally saw herself to be a strongly social-service oriented person, one who could comfortably be a teacher or a social worker and feel that she was making a substantial contribution to mankind. At the same time, Carol was oriented toward getting married, having children and raising a family. In college she dated a great deal, had many friends, and got along well with peers of both sexes. She and her older brother, currently a law student at another university some distance away, had a good relationship.

Carol's presenting problem was vague. She felt mildly depressed but she could not clearly identify the antecedents of the depression. Her operational description of her mild depression was that she found herself sighing frequently, often felt "blue" (emotionally drained) and frequently found herself thinking a great deal about questions concerning what she would do with her life and what kind of life would be worthwhile to live. Her conversations with friends centered about questions concerning appropriate sexual behavior, whether or not to use drugs such as marijuana, LSD, etc. She found herself considering a great many of the moral questions of the culture in the area of civil rights and relations with authority figures. She found that after these conversations, she felt depressed (i.e., lethargic, with a sense of heaviness in her chest and unresponsive to stimuli). She had many questions, few answers: she was not at all sure that she wanted to live the sort of life her parents had led, or continue to be a member of the affluent society. At the same time, she was able to recognize that she enjoyed the material benefits of that society while feeling some mild guilt about accepting them. What she said she hopes to accomplish in counseling was to have an opportunity to talk with someone outside her immediate circle of friends about these concerns and perhaps, as a consequence, work out some acceptable value system and way of life. She felt her friends could not be helpful to her because they were wrestling with the same sort of problems and many of them took a condemning attitude toward her for admitting that she did enjoy nice clothes, a nice house, cars, travel, etc.

Behavioral analysis for counseling

Analysis of the problem behavior. The problem behavior was not clear. The closest the counselor could come to specifying it was in connection with the series of depressive episodes (mentioned earlier) that Carol experienced as well as the series of ruminative thoughts about questions of life values.

Analysis of the problem situation. Carol's problem situation was more than the result of being in college at a particular place and moment in time, although that obviously contributed a great deal to her discomfort. On a subjective level, Carol seemed to be experiencing a developmental problem that many young women of her age in our culture at this time are experiencing. This problem centered about the identification of a set of values to live by. Consequently, her counselor could not seriously consider any situational manipulation or superficial change of education program to help Carol since the problem would remain with her despite changes in her life's setting in the immediate future.

The analysis of the educational-vocational environment. There is no question that being a college student was adding to Carol's difficulties in identifying a clear set of values for herself. Her readings, academic lectures and friends, all made her challenge values which she formerly either had held without thinking about them seriously, or which she had formerly agreed with actively. Now, however, many of her early assumptions were challenged, leaving her for the moment, at least, without any orienting structure on which to base her behavior. Thus, it was, in a way, Carol's educational-vocational environment which was exacerbating her difficulties while, paradoxically perhaps, at the same time offered the means by which she could solve her difficulties.

The analysis of the family environment. Carol's family understood neither the questions that Carol was riasing nor her reasons for raising them. Not surprisingly, Carol's father could not understand his daughter's rejection of his values. He had worked hard to develop a good business as a building contractor and made a good income which provided a comfortable style of life for his family. Thus, it angered him to find that his daughter did not appreciate the many benefits he had provided for her. Carol's mother, while somewhat more tolerant of Carol's inability to accept without question the material benefits her father had provided, was concerned about Carol's behavior. She was afraid that Carol would engage in excessive sexual behavior or experiment with drugs and, thus, be either injured by drug use, or become pregnant. Carol's brother, while having gone through a similar episode himself only a few years before, was now so deeply engrossed in his law studies and new marriage that he could provide little help to Carol in finding her way. The family environment thus added stress to Carol's situation. Carol managed the stress reasonably well, mainly because she was distant physically and emotionally from home. She rarely visited home; when she did, she found those periods immediately prior to and subsequent to home visits were ones of somewhat more intense depression than usual. These visits precipitated an increased awareness of the discrepancy between her views and those of her family.

Interpersonal relations. Carol had a very busy social and sexual life. She dated every weekend and sometimes during the week. These dates were often informal, where several couples would heatedly discuss social issues of the time. Occasionally, there was a party on the weekend, or Carol and her date would attend some musical or theatrical event that the university was sponsoring. Usually, the evenings ended with Carol slightly drunk and slightly aroused sexually as a result of some mild to moderate heterosexual play. On several occasions, Carol had engaged in sexual relations with her date, afterwards feeling some guilt. Her guilt and anxiety were shortlived, however, and evidenced itself only as she continued to express questions about what effects this might have on her later marital adjustment.

The group that she associated with would also occasionally experiment with marijuana but Carol had thus far abstained from that experimentation, fearing the consequences of being caught by college or civil authorities.

As a consequence, it can be seen that Carol's social and sexual environment heaped fuel on the fires of her value conflict. In her social life, she was increasingly being drawn into a pattern of behavior that was in conflict with the pattern of behavior she had been taught to value at home.

The analysis of thinking process responses. In many ways, the nub of Carol's problem rested in her thoughts about her social and sexual behaviors. She found herself thinking about her value conflicts to a great extent. The only times she was not preoccupied with value questions were those times when she was in class, absorbed in the content of her course work. However, outside of class, even while she was studying, thoughts about the value conflict would intrude. Since Carol was very capable academically, her grades did not suffer, and she was able to maintain her Dean's list academic performance. Carol, however, wanted counseling specifically about those matters which preoccupied her. She wanted to talk about these things.

Biological and physical attributes. Carol appeared to be in good health and had more than adequate recreational outlets (as indicated in the section on social and sexual environment).

Counseling goals and strategies

On the basis of the behavioral analysis the counselor concluded it would not be relevant to attempt to have Carol change her style of life since she was really interested in coming to grips first with the question of what style of life she wanted to lead. Once that question was partially resolved, at least, then she could begin to face the question of what, if any, changes in the way she behaved would be desirable. What Carol really seemed to need was an opportunity for extensive and intensive discussions with the counselor, during which time she could explore her questions, guilts, concerns over her sexual activities, her lack of vocational direction, and her failure to identify a reasonably acceptable life goal for herself. In essence, the counselor was using a supportive strategy to foster the client's development through a difficult developmental period. This case thus represents a way the facilitative-affective approach to a problem might be used in counseling.

Carol was seen by her counselor on a weekly basis for the remaining part of her sophomore year and through the entire junior year. These sessions were not highly structured and allowed Carol to talk freely about the wide range of concerns mentioned earlier. During this time Carol did not completely come to grips with all of the questions that she had at the outset, but she was able to come to the important recognition that the concerns she had could not be quickly answered and would be developmentally resolved. She also began to accept the fact that continuation in her current style of behavior would probably lead to an unwelcome confrontation with her parents and, possibly, with society. As a result, she began to move away from excessive social rebellion and began to moderate her sexual activities. She continued to refuse to become engaged in the use of drugs, and she did not entirely give up all of her sexual activities, but became more concerned with the emotional relationships with the young men she dated than with the sexual aspects of the relationships. She became more selective about her sexual partners. At the time the counselor concluded working with Carol, she was dating one student regularly; this relationship appeared to be heading toward marriage. As a consequence, many of her sexual concerns were receding, since she was able to resolve some of her guilt over her sexual intimacies with this young man in the context of the anticipated marriage.

Carol's mild depression remained, but seemed to be somewhat moderated because of the outlet the counselor provided for her emotional concerns.

Summary. This case shows how the facilitative-affective counseling approach may be used in helping a student through a difficult developmental problem exacerbated by the culture. While the outcome was not clear, over the period of time the counselor worked with Carol, her distress was somewhat alleviated and her behavior became less likely to lead to long-term disruption. The counselor wisely refrained from trying to help Carol restructure her life abruptly, because Carol did not perceive the problem in the same terms as did the counselor. Carol needed a period of time to enable herself to come to terms with her social values and did not seem likely to respond well to a structuring of social values imposed on her by the counselor. In fact, it seemed that she had gotten into her difficulty largely because she was rejecting a set of values that had been imposed on her by her parents. As a result, the counselor had little choice but to follow a facilitative-affective strategy in working with Carol. As a consequence, he provided a useful service by helping Carol move a little further down the road toward resolving the large questions that faced her as well as helping her to avoid getting excessively involved in anti-social behaviors which might have unnecessarily complicated her life later.

CLEM

Clem was an eighteen-year-old freshman at Ginger College, majoring in Chemistry when he first saw a counselor. He was a good-looking young man with average dress and grooming. Though not a verbally fluent person, Clem was able to report that he was anxious about his interpersonal relationships, particularly with girls.

Clem's father was a hard-working farmer of modest means who lived for

the most part by the Protestant ethic—honesty and hard work. He was not
a verbal man and rarely attended social activities. The mother's life was
restricted primarily to the home and church activities. In high school, Clem
studied hard and was graduated with a high scholastic average. He attended
few social functions, did not date, and was not active in sports. Most of his
free time was devoted to helping out on the farm. He had no brothers or
sisters.

Clem lived in a single room in a residence hall at Ginger College.
During the autumn quarter he studied seriously and did well scholastically.
He did not date during the fall but he did become acquainted with two
other freshmen students majoring in chemistry who lived in the residence
hall. In general, Clem's daily schedule involved classes, study, and recreational activities such as watching the stock market and listening to popular
music. Clem's activities were solitary and involved little interaction with
others.

Clem's reason for coming to the counseling center involved his anxiety
about dating. His first date in high school was for the senior prom. His
partner was very moralistic, aggressive, and domineering. Clem was not
socially skilled, nor did he know how to dance. In the company of another
couple, his date referred to Clem as a social slob and she left the dance alone.
This experience severely embarrassed Clem and made him feel extremely
inadequate personally and socially. He had not had a date since. Moreover,
he had since tended to avoid females where possible.

Clem's major interpersonal orientation seemed to be one of movement
away from people. Test data from the Adjective Check List further suggested
that Clem was high in needs deference and abasiveness.

Behavior analysis for counseling

Clarification of the problem behavior. Clem was concerned about his interpersonal
relationships, specifically his heterosexual relationships. He wanted to be
able to talk comfortably with females and date casually. In the company of
girls Clem reported withdrawn behavior, he felt flushed, his hands perspired,
and he found it extremely difficult to talk. In addition, he escaped from the
situation as soon as possible. In general, Clem perceived himself as being
awkward and inadequate socially.

Clarification of the problem situation. Clem was concerned about his lacks of
skill in interacting with females. His difficulty seemed to be the result of
his limited opportunity to learn social behavior in combination with his
single extremely traumatic heterosexual experience. For the most part, his
efforts at social behavior had not been rewarding. Upon entering college and
leaving home, his perceived social inadequacy increased because the more he

wanted to date, the more the thought of approaching a girl made him anxious. Thus, his conflict increased. Clem managed his anxiety level by minimizing interactions with females, although his social dissatisfaction remained.

Analaysis of the educational or work environment. The reduction of Clem's inability to be effective with girls was expected to improve his academic effectiveness. Clem's educational environment encouraged the acquisition of adaptive social behaviors. It was possible to identify certain reinforcing stimuli in school that could facilitate social behaviors. One such reinforcing event was Clem's satisfaction in being away from home. In addition, Clem's academic work was satisfactory and he liked his first quarter as a chemistry major. Still another reinforcing stimulus was Clem's adviser who was a source of encouragement. Clem mentioned his social concern to his adviser who suggested he seek help at the counseling center.

A hierarchy of aversive stimuli related to Clem's educational environment was also observed. One aversive stimulus was Clem's tendency to over-study and prepare excessively for academic courses. Studying hard and long was effective to a point, but for Clem it contributed to social inexperience. Clem also had difficulty participating actively in class. He would become very anxious when attempting to ask a question or present an opinion and, as a result, generally refrain from doing so.

Analysis of the family environment. Little in Clem's family environment supported the acquisition of polished social behaviors. Clem's parents were oriented to hard work and preparation for expected future bad times. According to their view, a person should feel guilty if he enjoyed life too much. As a youth Clem had adopted this attitude of his parents, but he was now questioning it because his new surroundings enabled him to see the value of being socially competent and enjoying life. As a result, like many students, he had begun to question some attitudes that he acquired from his parents.

Interpersonal relationships. A positive reinforcing stimulous in Clem's social environment was the relationship he developed with two other freshmen majoring in chemistry and living in his residence hall. These three young men frequently attended meals together and often studied as a group. These friendships revealed that Clem could get along adequately with males. They thus reassured him about his social adequacy to some degree. A second socially reinforcing stimulus involve Clem's interests in the stock market and in music. These areas of interest offered potential social value to him because they provided vehicles for interesting conversation.

The aversive hierarchy included Clem's thoughts about his failure to have ever been involved in any kind of significant relationship with a female during his life. His sexual need was satisfied by masturbation over which he periodically became guilty and anxious. Clem's difficulties in making friends was exacerbated by the fact that he had a single room in the residence hall which reduced the frequency of spontaneous socializing.

Analysis of the thinking process. Clem accurately perceived himself to be socially ineffective with females. Consequently, he avoided situations and relationships which involved females in order to keep his anxiety low. He wanted to date but when he thought about dating he became intensely anxious. He wanted to change his pattern of thinking and his behavior, he wanted to be able to be comfortable in talking with and dating females, but his thoughts about girls always increased his anxiety to an uncomfortable level. A major amount of his time was spent ruminating over his lack of ability to get along with girls.

Biological and physical attributes. A recent physical examination taken for the college indicated that Clem's physical condition was satisfactory. He was not athletically inclined but he frequently took long walks. In addition, he was enrolled in the college's compulsory physical education program. These activities kept him in satisfactory physical condition. Clem's recreational choices were solitary in nature, thus further contributing to his lack of social experience.

Goals and strategies

An abbreviated behavior modification strategy was implemented in working with Clem. As might be expected the goals of this strategy were the reduction of anxiety associated with females, the acquisition of social skills and behaviors, and the implementation of these behaviors.

To accomplish the goal of anxiety reduction, Clem was encouraged to talk about his anxiety feelings associated with his initial dating experience in high school and with females in general. In talking about his previous experiences with females (anxiety provoking stimulus), Clem actually experienced anxiety as he reviewed specific situations. However, in the counselor-client relationship the anxiety was not reinforced and Clem's anxiety associated with thoughts of females was gradually reduced. For example, this process (desensitization) eliminated Clem's perspiring of the hands when thinking or talking about females.

The next goal involved the acquisition of new behavior (acquiring social skills and behaviors). In order to accumulate some information in this area Clem enrolled in a social etiquette course taught by the Home Economics Department. His attention was brought to expected behaviors and attitudes in social situations. In addition, Clem had indirect contact with females in this class, something his chemistry curriculum normally worked against.

The behavior acquisition goal was divided into a series of sub-goals. First, the counselor suggested Clem find a roommate and move out of his single room. This change alone increased the frequency of his interaction with people. A second sub-goal involved increasing his contacts with females. After some desensitization interviews, Clem was able to smile and say hello to girls he knew when he saw them on campus. Clem was eventually able to make this small interpersonal overture without becoming overly anxious. Then, Clem was encouraged by the counselor to talk with a coed after class. To make this possible Clem was assigned a structured situation. He asked a female classmate for missing class information. After repeating this behavior on several occasions, he was able to begin talking about other topics (academic courses, the college football team, current events) but the topic continued to be highly structured. In counseling Clem discussed his feelings of anxiety in implementing these behaviors and again, a desensitization process was used to reduce his anxiety. The sequence was repeated several times with several girls. Eventually Clem was able to casually walk from one class to another with a female. This result he found to be quite satisfying. However, he remained anxious about spending more than short periods with a female. As the winter quarter closed Clem was satisfied with his progress so far.

During the vacation an unplanned event occurred. While visiting a high school teacher he met a female student, also majoring in chemistry at another college. Since the two of them had the subject of chemistry in common, they talked easily for some time. They accidentally met a second time while shopping in town and again talked for some 30 minutes. Clem's confidence in talking with females increased immensely as a result of these two encounters. In general, his level of anxiety was lower and he began to talk with the counselor about dating.

In the spring quarter Clem suggested, and the counselor reinforced, the idea of enrolling in a dance class. This further increased his contact with females and introduced the notion of physical contact, albeit minimal, for the first time. In addition, he was able to acquire another social skill. The next sub-goal, structured by the counselor, involved a "coke date" after one of the dancing classes. Clem implemented this plan with Sue and reported little anxiety. He liked Sue and felt comfortable being with her. Clem now was prepared to date. He suggested taking Sue to a residence hall dance and the counselor reinforced this response. He took Sue to the dance and enjoyed himself.

Clem eventually began to interact with females with some spontaneity. He reported feeling comfortable with females and a desire to be with them. The counselor next discussed with Clem the idea of taking a course in the area of marriage and family. In addition, Clem was encouraged to do some reading in the area of sex education. The counseling sessions were reduced to one each month in case Clem felt the need to talk with someone, and soon Clem terminated his counseling, finding his need for assistance diminished.

Summary. Clem, an eighteen-year-old freshman, came to the counseling center and reported that he was anxious in interpersonal relationships with females. He wanted to be able to talk comfortably with females and date casually. In general, Clem preceived himself to be awkward and inadequate socially. His difficulty was, to some degree, the result of a limited opportunity to learn social behavor. A modified desensitization technique was used in working with Clem. The goals of strategy used were the reduction of anxiety associated with females, the acquisition of social skills and behaviors, and the implementation of these behaviors. Clem needed an active counselor, one ready to introduce new social skills and concepts to his client and help in their acquisition.

This case illustrates how a desensitization procedure can be useful in working with an individual whose anxiety is specific and traumatically precipitated. For Clem the traumatic event found fertile ground because he had no offsetting experiences to counter it, and, thus, the second part of the counselor's strategy was to help Clem accumulate a reservoir of good experiences with girls to offset any future rejections.

HUSTON

Huston was a twenty-three-year-old high school drop-out when he first saw a counselor at Northern College. Huston was a clean, neat, good-looking young man, who expressed himself clearly and indicated that he wanted to go to college. Huston was living with his brother in the city. His father was employed as a grocery store clerk and his mother, besides being a housewife, worked part time as a waitress. James, Huston's brother, had graduated from high school and was now successfully employed as a mason. There were no other children in the family.

At age 17, Huston dropped out of high school (junior year) and enlisted in the Navy for four years. He performed at an average level while in school. In the service he was assigned to a gun crew; consequently, he had no specialized training that would transfer to a civilian occupation. After being honorably discharged from the Navy, he worked as a maintenance man for a small business for one year. This job involved mainly the repair of equipment. He grew dissatisfied with the job because it required little interaction with people and was not intellectually demanding. He therefore looked for a better job, but found his efforts to be fruitless considering his level of education. He finally accepted a job driving a potato chip truck, but soon became dissatisfied once again.

Huston's reason for coming to the counseling center involved his desire to attend college. More specifically, he was interested in exploring his academic potential and interests. He wanted to know if he could be admitted to a college without a high school diploma. If admitted to a college, the government would financially sponsor his education. Huston's test scores on the ACT suggested average academic potential for college. The Strong Vocational Interest Blank reflected a primary interest pattern in the Business Contact area.

Behavior analysis for counseling

Clarification of the problem behavior. Huston was concerned about exploring his abilities and interests. He had been dissatisfied with the service and his two previous jobs. He wanted to be an educated man, and perceived himself as possessing sufficient intelligence to complete a college degree.

The data suggested that Huston had not been aware of the value of a college degree when he dropped out of high school. Furthermore, he had little formal educational training since, and consequently his response repertoire did not include many effective educational responses. In essence, Huston wanted a college degree in order to improve his position in life. He desired to acquire the thought processes and behaviors of a man prepared to function in a professional vocation.

Clarification of the problem situation. So far Huston had been unhappy and dissatisfied in the world of work. Through past experiences he realized that he wanted to be intellectually involved in his work and saw an opportunity to accomplish this only through higher education. A natural outgrowth of this was Huston's concern about his educational-behavioral deficit. Huston was further impelled to action by his strong desire for material things. These two objectives were in conflict with his desire to obtain immediate rather than delayed rewards and reinforcement.

Analysis of the educational or work environment. Huston's work environment encouraged his ideas about returning to school to learn a job related skill. In his mind education had become increasingly related to occupational advancement. The college degree was seen to be a required credential for nearly all vocational pursuits he viewed to be worthwhile. Huston saw that this response deficit had to be modified if he were to improve his vocational position.

In analyzing Huston's work environment, it was possible to identify a significant antecedent. One such event was Huston's dissatisfaction with the military service and his two previous jobs. He had found all three of these vocational tasks to be intellectually shallow and financially unrewarding.

A number of factors related to Huston's work environment reinforced his desire to return to school. One such reinforcing stimulus was that his boss at the potato chip company encouraged him to think he could complete additional education. In addition, through his previous work experiences, Huston realized that he wanted to be intellectually involved in his work and that he wanted to work and be with people in a competitive, interpersonally manipulative environment where he could advance on the basis of his own skills rather than expect institutional rewards. He did not want to work away from other people. The availability of government financial support for educational expenses throught the GI bill further reinforced his desire to return to school.

Analysis of the family environment. The family environment did not affect Huston's acquisition of further education one way or another. His parents had questioned the value of a college education, but it was their desire that Huston finish high school. Huston had introjected his parents' attitude originally, but because of his work experiences since leaving home he was now questioning it. One positive family stimulus was that Huston's brother, whom he admired, had encouraged him to return to school. James also suggested that Huston could continue to live at home for a reduced rent fee while going to school.

Interpersonal relationships. A positive reinforcing stimulus in Huston's social environment was the relationship he had developed with a female college graduate (Elaine) employed as a nurse. Huston had been dating Elaine for the past year. She encouraged Huston's pursuit of a college degree.

Aversive stimuli included Huston's lack of a high school diploma. Huston feared the lack of a diploma might doom his efforts to earn a degree since it was bound to influence his admission to a college. Blocked from enrolling in college, Huston would have little opportunity to enter social groups which attracted him.

Analysis of the thinking process. Huston perceived himself to be intellectually competent and capable of pursuing and completing a college degree. At the same time he was concerned about the effects his inadequate training would have on his ability to compete successfully for a desired vocational position. He had been unhappy and dissatisfied in his previous jobs and was counting on a college degree to help him obtain a better position. Huston's analysis of the situation seemed realistic to the counselor.

Biological and physical attributes. A recent physical examination for a previous job indicated that Huston's physical condition was satisfactory. Huston regularly exercised at the local Y.M.C.A. two nights a week, usually running and swimming. He enjoyed regular physical exercise.

Goals and strategies

The strategy used in working with Huston was a combination of decision making and behavior modification. The goals were the assessment of Huston's academic potential, admission to a college or university, selection of a college major, and the acquisition of effective study behaviors.

Since Huston's intellectual potential was congruent with his educational goal, his counselor encouraged him to write letters of inquiry regarding college admissions. In particular, Huston wanted to attend Northern College, a local school. The fact that Huston did not possess a high school diploma was obviously a problem. He had been recently informed by high school officials that it would take him approximately two years to complete a high school course. Consequently, Huston had decided to attempt to enter college without the diploma, a decision which the counselor reinforced. The counselor and Huston agreed that the two years in high school would be of no practical value.

After an interview with the Admissions Office at Northern College, Huston was informed that he could be admitted to the college for the summer quarter on academic probation if he earned a high school diploma by passing the General Educational Development Test. This was arranged.

The next goal involved the selection of a college major. Since the Strong Vocational Interest Blank reflected a primary interest pattern in the Business Contact area suggesting interests similar to individuals in sales management, real estate sales, and life insurance sales, Huston sought occupational information about those fields. Eventually he tentatively decided to major in business administration. This potential college major also seemed to be congruent with his intellectual ability. The jobs resulting from a business administration major, emphasizing assertive interpersonal relations seemed very suitable to Huston. The work involved variety and was sufficiently intellectually demanding to satisfy Huston.

The counselor suggested that Huston use the spring quarter to acquire and develop effective study behaviors. He pursued this objective by enrolling in a study skills program offered by the Counseling Center at Northern College. In addition, he enrolled in a reading improvement course offered through the college's continuing education program. During the summer quarter, Huston enrolled in basic courses in history, English, mathematics, and pyschology. He earned three B's and one C. As a result, he was admitted as a regular, full-time undergraduate student for the autumn quarter in business administration.

Summary. Huston's reason for coming to the counseling center involved his desire to attend college. Specifically, he was interested in exploring his academic potential and interests. He had been dissatisfied with the military service and his two previous jobs. Huston did not have a high school diploma but perceived himself as being bright enough to earn a college degree. The approach used in working with Huston was a combination of decision making and behavior modification. The goals of this strategy involved an analysis of Huston's academic potential, admission to a college or university, the selection of a college major, and the acquisition of effective study behaviors.

While one element in Huston's case is distinctive, that is, his lack of a high school diploma, the assessment and counseling task used with Huston represents a common set of counseling objectives and operations. The goals are concrete, the methods direct and largely cognitive, and the counseling brief.

SUE

Sue was a nineteen-year-old freshman when she first saw her counselor at the college counseling center. Sue, a neatly dressed, attractive Black young woman, reported that she was concerned about her tendency to become extremely anxious and tense. When anxious she developed headaches, found the palms of her hands perspiring, and withdrew from the environment. To Sue certain situations seemed to produced the anxiety responses.

Three types of events seemed to antedate her anxiety. Criticism of any sort made her very anxious; she became extremely tense when thinking about her life goals (she strongly felt the need to decide on a college major); and, thirdly, Sue seemed to have difficulty in expressing her anger. When she became angry she would withdraw from the situation rather than act upon her anger, which added to her physical tension.

Sue was living at home in a small apartment with her mother. Her father was dead and her mother supported the family by working as a waitress in an exclusive restaurant. Sue contributed financially while in high school by working as a car hop.

In high school Sue's academic performance was about B+, consistent with her slightly above average scores on the ACT examination. Upon completing high school she worked for one year as a clerk in a grocery store in order to make money to pay for her first year of college. She was undecided about her college major choice, but expressed tentative interest in nursing. During her first quarter at the college in a general liberal arts program her academic performance was in the C+ range.

Socially Sue was active. She was dating two young men both enrolled in the college. Sue enjoyed being with both these men, but did not want to get too involved with either one. She wanted to complete her college degree before getting married.

Test data from the Minnesota Multiphasic Personality Inventory showed an above average score on the psychasthenic scale. This result was consistent with Sue's reported excessive worry and anxiety. The Strong Vocational Interest Blank reflected no primary interest pattern. Sue was caught between wanting the secure comfort of a vocationally oriented program and the desire to study a widely ranging array of courses.

Behavior analysis for counseling

Clarification of problem behavior. Sue was concerned about her tendency to respond in an anxious and tense manner in certain situations. She wanted to be able to function without severe anxiety responses. The specific behaviors associated with the anxiety response included headache, perspiring of the palms of the hands, and withdrawal from the environment. These behavioral excesses were coupled with a behavioral deficit: Sue was not able to express her anger overtly. When anxious she withdrew from interpersonal situations.

Clarification of the problem situation. Sue's excessive anxiety responses seemed to occur when she perceived herself to be criticized; the anxiety was not restricted to any one setting, but school was a context in which critical evaluation by others is the order of the day. In addition, she grew anxious when she thought about her life goals. For example, she thought she should be preparing for a specific occupation in college but had not yet identified one. Through counseling Sue desired to reduced or eliminate the anxiety responses associated with these situations. Further, she wanted to make a decision about her future and reduce her fear of being evaluated.

Analysis of the educational or work environment. Though Sue's academic performance during her first quarter in college was satisfactory, she thought she could improve her performance. She was not dissatisfied with the liberal arts program, but she wanted to select a college major. She related her concerns to her academic adviser who suggested that she come to the counseling center.

A further analysis of Sue's educational setting revealed some specific anxiety-producing situations. The written comments made by her instructor on her themes in English class stimulated an anxiety-anger-withdrawal response sequence. Evaluative comments of her work made in class, instigated the same pattern. Sue thus did not profit from criticism since she withdrew from it. In general, stimuli in the educational environment that Sue perceived to be critical elicited the same, self-defeating response pattern.

Analysis of the family environment. Her mother actively supported Sue's educational efforts. Though her income was limited she helped to finance

Sue's education. At the same time, Sue's mother placed a high value on the practical aspects of higher education and, consequently, pressed Sue to select a college major. Her mother's insistence on narrowing her field contributed to Sue's anxiety. Sue wanted to make some educational-vocational decision in order to reduce the pressure and implied criticism from her mother.

Interpersonal relationships. Sue was active and successful socially. She enjoyed dating the two young men mentioned earlier. In addition, relationships with other girls, both negro and white, were rewarding and satisfying. However, if a peer made an evaluative response about her, her anxiety began to rise. For example, if a boyfriend mentioned that he did not like her hair style, or disagreed with her opinion on some current issue, the anxiety-anger-withdrawal sequence was elicited. In another social realm, friends of Sue's mother frequently made her uncomfortable and angry by inquiring about her college major.

Analysis of the thinking process. Sue over-perceived comments from others indicating their rejection of her. She anticipated rejection from others inappropriately. Consequently, her responses were often inappropriate and she engaged in social withdrawal behaviors excessively. To reduce the frequency of occurrence of the anxiety pattern Sue had begun to avoid people. She was aware of the undesirability of this coping technique and was concerned about her behavior. In addition, Sue found she avoided novel situations because of her anticipatory fears of rejection. She perceived most critical comments to imply inadequacy on her part.

Biological and physical attributes. A physical examination prior to college entrance indicated Sue's physical condition to be satisfactory and revealed no physical basis for her headaches.

Goals and strategies

The strategy used in working with Sue was a combination of behavior modification and decision-making. Its goals were first, the reduction of anxiety associated with the evaluative remarks of others and, second, the selection of a college major.

To accomplish the goal of anxiety reduction, desensitization coupled with relaxation was used. During the first three hours the counselor collected data enabling him to construct a hierarchy of anxiety-producing stimuli. The hierarchy included the following ranked from low to high in anxiety production:

1) A student is reading an essay on folk music that you have written.

2) The student reading the essay is frowning and shaking her head.

3) The student reading the essay is writing comments in the margins of the paper.

4) The student drops the paper saying that she never did like folk music.

To aid the relaxation process Sue sat in a comfortable lounge chair with her eyes shut. Then, with the counselor's aid Sue was encouraged to relax the various parts of her body. The counselor mentioned each part of the body from the head to the toes and Sue concentrated on relaxing.

When Sue was in a relaxed state the first stimulus was introduced. If the stimulus produced anxiety Sue was instructed to move her right fore-finger. The relaxation procedure created an antagonistic response to the anxiety response in the face of the stimulus. In this way, Sue gradually progressed through the hierarchy. Outside of the counseling session she was encouraged to implement the relaxation technique if she began to feel anxious.

However, Sue reported that this procedure did not seem to help when she felt personally rejected. Consequently, a second hierarchy of anxiety producing stimuli was developed. This hierarchy was more interpersonally oriented and involved the following steps:

1) Your boyfriend is staring at you.

2) Your boyfriend mentions that he doesn't care for the shoes you are wearing.

3) Your boyfriend mentions that he doesn't like your hair style.

4) Your boyfriend mentions that you seem to be in a bad mood.

The same relaxation procedure was used with this hierarchy as earlier. Eventually Sue was able to move through this hierarchy without becoming anxious. In reducing the anxiety response, the anger and withdrawal behavior sequence was disrupted and, consequently, anger and withdrawal were also reduced. In addition, through discussions in the interview, Sue gradually began to learn to discriminate between aggressive responses made to hurt her and constructive responses intended to aid her. In acquiring this understanding she realized that she should respond differently to these different situations. In role playing with the counselor she learned some techniques enabling her to cope with the hostile responses of others. She took the view, for example, that if a boyfriend didn't like her hair style that was his problem, not hers. In general, after seeing Sue weekly for four months, she seemed more realistic, less anxious, and less guarded interpersonally. She was more willing to engage in new behaviors in novel situations; for example, she attempted to ski for the first time in her life. Sue's overall social and intellectual functioning seemed to be more effective.

Attention was now directed toward the next goal, the selection of a college major. The interview was used to canvass Sue's expressed vocational interests. Sue showed some mild interest in the nursing program which led to a bachelor's degree, and thus would allow her to pursue her liberal arts interests while at the same time equip her with a marketable vocational skill with which to satisfy her mother and her own concerns about security. Sue decided to take two introductory courses in the nursing program in the Autumn Quarter.

Summary. Sue, nineteen-year-old freshman, reported concern about her tendency to become extremely anxious. The anxiety responses seemed to occur when Sue was being evaluated and when she contemplated her life goals. The first strategy used in working with Sue involved a behavior modification technique called desensitization in which the reduction of anxiety associated with evaluative remarks was accomplished by teaching Sue to relax in the presence of anxiety provoking thoughts, thus interfering with the anxiety sequence and its results. The second phase involved the selection of a college major which satisfied Sue's need to maintain wide interests and at the same time complete college with a specific vocational skill.

SUMMARY

The cases described in Part II have been presented to accomplish several objectives. First, an effort was made to illustrate a wide and typical range of problems brought to counselors operating in institutional settings. Second, the cases have been used to demonstrate concepts of behavioral and environmental analysis. Third, through the cases we have strived to illustrate the application of the conceptions of the four conseling strategies presented in Part I of this book. The cases have varied with respect to the degree of intervention versus facilitative focus and cognitive versus affective content. Though the overall approach taken by the counselors represents the interventionistic-cognitive viewpoint some affective and facilitative techniques were used. In one case, Carol, the affective-facilitative approach predominated. Fourth, the cases have attempted to illustrate the advantages of different counseling for different problems, along with the use of specifically tailored behavioral criteria to aid in evaluating case outcome, rather than the use of a single approach to all problems and comprehensive criteria. Finally, the cases have been designed to illustrate the need to specify goals in counseling.

The case of Carl and his grief reaction has shown the creative use to which support in counseling may be put in halting and reversing what was fundamentally a normal reaction to a natural event that got out of hand. The result was attained quickly—time was important. Other approaches, more reflective and facilitative in nature, would have emphasized the acquisition of coping responses slower to have impact on Carl. It is reasonable to question the likelihood of a desirable case outcome had Carl been permitted to remain in his depressive state for a prolonged period.

Harry, the schizoid student, shows how good use can be made of some responses of even a self-deprecating client. It also illustrates vividly how the implementation of an obvious but incorrect counseling plan would lead to an undesirable outcome for the client, making the point that clients can be injured by the application of inappropriate treatment as well as by leaving them alone.

Bart, illustrating the use of a performance improvement strategy, (externalizing study responses) stands in sharp contrast to the approach used in working with Harry. Harry's academic inadequacies were a function of his inability to attend to his studies, the inability itself the result of social antecedents. Bart, on the other hand, had never learned effective study methods; furthermore, his motivation to learn to study was high, and the antecedents to his poor attention were cognitive, not affective like Harry's.

The case of the homesick freshman, Ed, represents the way several strategies can be used together. If counseling plan A results in outcome B, then strategy C would follow; if strategy A results in outcome B prime, then strategy C prime would be the plan of choice. If Ed had not developed well in his academic environment (strategy A) then the counselor would have modified the strategy to follow. This type of approach permits the counselor to plan casework but does not rigidly commit him to subsequent strategies which are later proven to be undesirable.

For Ann, caught in the throes of choice anxiety, still another combination of strategies is illustrated. Here, support was used to tide her through a difficult period after first using a behavior-modification technique to make it possible for her to enter the fearful situation in which she was to receive still further support.

Lethargic Bob shows how careful a counselor must be to avoid concluding that all behavior problems that come his way have a psychological basis. Bob's problem had psychological concomitants, but these were outcomes rather than antecedents. Attention to outcomes, changes neither the antecedent nor the consequent events. Verbal or behavioral counseling with Bob would have been futile.

The case describing Ray's problems shows how a combination of behavior-modification and decision-making strategies work together. Ray's anxiety with respect to a decision-making task was subjected to a modified desensitization, following which new and assertive decision-making behaviors were acquired. The extinction of the old, anxiety responses made it more feasible for Ray to learn his new assertive skills. The counselor took a major role in urging Ray to try new, assertive behaviors.

Similarly, for Clem, a modified anxiety reducing desensitization strategy was applied to enable him to engage in new social responses where a major role of the counselor was that of coach and trainer.

A somewhat complicated educational-vocational counseling case representing the cognitive-interventionistic approach can be observed in the case of Huston. Huston knew the level of his educational objective but the counselor introduced the means, the content, and taught him some of the basic skills necessary to implement his eventual choice.

Carol's situation stands as a subjectively oriented, facilitative-affective case, where the client's problem represents an exaggeration of a normal difficulty in developing social and personal values. The cognitive-interventionistic approach would be of little, if any, value in working with a student like Carol during this period of her life in connection with the concerns she presented.

Finally, Sue's situation illustrates the use of desensitization applied to reduce interpersonal anxiety directly, a sopposed to the indirect approach of insight counseling.

The reader is reminded that these case representations are not designed to prove the method described in this book. Cases can only illustrate, not prove, an approach. These cases, composites of casework with real clients, do show how behavioral analysis can be used in understanding client behavior, in planning counseling procedures, and in setting outcome objectives that are specially tailored to the individual client.

PART 3

Chapter 6

Issues

It is curious how counseling, developed to provide individual attention to people whose institutions otherwise treat them programmatically in groups, has so often become rigid in the service which it delivers. The argument against offering the services one can provide rather than those the client needs (Callis, 1961) has typically been overwhelmed by doctrinaire views insisting that all clients need one particular treatment. Pity the poor client whose own counseling objectives are buried in the avalanche of the counselor's needs, values, and skills. Naturally, the counselor must provide a service in which he has skill, and which seems reasonable to him. Nevertheless, rather than restrict his service narrowly, he should strive to broaden his conceptual and counseling skills to include as wide a variety of techniques and potential services as he can, all the while recognizing that where his limitations begin, another counselor's skills take over. Thus, this book has had as its objective, the illustration of ways to identify and specify a number of appropriate case management procedures that can be specifically tailored to client needs.

The management procedures suggested are dictated partly by the client problems, environmental and personal facilitators and deterrents, and counselor skills and techniques. To aid in the task of planning a counseling program, a schematic framework for environmental and behavioral analysis was suggested.

PROTECTING THE CLIENT

Because of the highly individualized effort that will result from improved case planning, the counselor will have a more potent impact on the client. Along with the desirable consequences of this increased potency, some cautions need to be expressed. Care must be taken to develop safeguards concerning the client's autonomy in order to protect him from excessive manipulation by the counselor. Counselors have typically and appropriately been worried about protecting the client from undue manipulation; these concerns become more substantial as counseling methods develop which have the potential of promoting significant objective and subjective changes in the client's behavior.

Where gross behavioral approaches to counseling are employed, the task of protecting the client is relatively simple because of the obvious nature of interpersonal control. An example of some of the safeguards that can be taken to preserve the integrity of the client's autonomy can be found in Ayllon and Azrin's (1968) report of the effects of managing the behavior of a hospital population through the presentation or withholding of tangible rewards. As part of their effort to protect the patients, Ayllon and Azrin took steps to insure the public nature of the experiment and the option of all patients to be released from the experimental situation at any time.

One might also raise the question about whether it is more ethical to be actively involved in another person's troubles or more appropriate to be aloof. Latané and Darley (1970, in press) have studied the phenomenon of involvement and non-involvement in social settings, identifying some of the variables associated with offering or withholding assistance. In counseling help may be offered or withheld, too. Is the counselor, who is privately aware of steps a client might take to alleviate some aspects of his distress, acting ethically when he withholds his understanding in the hope that the client, in time, will be better off by helping himself? Are there circumstances when "not helping" may be less ethical and more disruptive to a client than actively intervening? Most would agree that is so; disagreement occurs with respect to specifying the circumstances.

Krumboltz' (1966b) identification of goals for behavioral counseling leads to similar inferences about protecting the client. According to Krumboltz, counseling goals should be individually tailored to the client, behaviorally defined, and agreed to by the counselor and client. This process of specification contributes to the explication of counselor controls and thus enhances the client's chance to preserve his autonomy.

No cut and dried solutions to the ethics of involvement or non-involvement exist, but some guidelines for the application of interventionistic-cognitive counseling may be suggested. First, the objectives of counseling should be understood to be the result of an open and agreed upon method of intervention. The process of agreement should be one in which the client has a veto. That is to say, the client can refuse the treatment entirely, he can accept the goals but decline the method to achieve them, he can decline the goals but accept the general counseling method, or he can request counseling but reject both the goals and methods offered and solicit others. In other words, a client failing in school might refuse to consider the counselor's objective of identifying a new academic goal more consistent with his talents, and instead, insist on maintaining his current academic goal through improved methods. While his counselor might feel such a plan reduces the probability of success, he may enlist in the client's cause since it may be justified in terms of the client's subjective values. Where the objective required striving for improved study techniques the counselor would probably join the client. Where the client disagreed about the method to be followed and, instead, wanted the counselor to intervene in his curriculum inappropriately (drop required courses, teach him to cheat, etc.) the counselor would probably decline. In other words, while the client has a veto over the counselor goals and methods, the counselor, too, has an explicit say.

This type of client-counselor interaction, the setting of goals and sub-goals for counseling, seems more likely to protect the client from undue and inappropriate counselor manipulation than the less explicit goal setting characteristic of unsystematic counseling that fails to specify behaviorally related objectives. In unsystematic counseling goals "emerge". As a result the goals may be inconsistent from time to time, may be logically incompatible, and may reflect the objectives of the more potent partner in the dyad, the counselor. Behavioral goal setting seems closer than most approaches to resolving the paradox of requiring the client to accept an unstructured counseling situation against his will, while at the same time recognizing the possibility that some clients will appropriately require less structured, developmental counseling.

Counselor selection. A second way that clients can be protected is through careful selection of counselors. To date, no acceptable systematic criteria for counselor selection have been presented though many studies of ideal counselor characteristics have been conducted (Cottle and Lewis, 1954; Cottle, Lewis and Penney, 1954). Part of the reason for the lack of adequate criteria for counselor selection is the paucity of suitable criteria for counseling itself. It is difficult to find a basis for selection of counselors when the job itself hasn't been clearly defined. One of the implications of using counseling strategies is the better definition of the counseling task and criteria. The only well accepted criterion for counselor selection is academic in nature even though some investigators (notably Carkhuff, et al., 1968) have challenged the adequacy of academic criteria.

One inference to be drawn from the counseling strategies approach is the notion that effective counselors must be able to vary their counseling style according to the needs of the client. One group of investigators (Allen, Whiteley, et al., 1968) has related this kill to cognitive flexibility. Their results suggest that counselors differ in their skill to vary their performance and techniques in counseling, and, furthermore, that these differences may be related to counselor effectiveness. Were this hypothesis further validated, and the validity of the counseling strategies approach confirmed, cognitive flexibility could be added to scholastic ability as a dimension in counselor selection.

Still another personal dimension potentially useful in counselor selection is social intelligence. Intuitively, it seems likely that the ability to be interpersonally alert would be of immeasurable value in becoming an effective counselor. One reason why little use has been made of social intelligence in counselor selection has been the lack of an appropriate means of measurement. Guilford (1967), however, has published several tests of social intelligence which may prove to be useful additions to the list of criteria for counselor selection. Preliminary findings indicate that the social intelligence tests provide information about counselor characteristics that is different from that usually accumulated through the compilation of scholastic data such as college grades and Graduate Record Examination scores (Osipow and Walsh, 1970).

Counselor training. After the selection of potentially effective and responsible counselor trainees, the next step in insuring ethical and competent counseling is teaching the prospective counselors not only the "why" of counseling, which tends to be highly emphasized in current training programs, but also the "how" of counseling. Too often it is assumed either that the trainees already possess certain basic counseling skills, such as the ability to listen carefully, and the ability to ask sensible behavioral questions, or that they will naturally acquire these skills over time without special attention. Such a view is shortsighted and does not give the trainee a fair chance.

Ignoring instruction in basic techniques of counseling may have been justified on technical grounds until recently. Now, however, a technology for instruction in small, specific, and important skills appears to be emerging, if only in rudimentary form. The work of Ivey and his colleagues (1968) using microcounseling to teach beginning counselors basic interviewing techniques illustrates the imaginative use to which principles of learning can be applied. In counselor training underlying the use of such techniques, however, is the acceptance of the view that skill in counseling technique is important. Such use assumes that while counselor understanding is important, even essential, in developing a counseling relationship that will promote client growth and effectiveness, relationships alone are not sufficient to bring about significant client change. Without the application of suitable counselor techniques, the potential of counseling to contribute to personal growth will never be achieved.

While the microcounseling approach might be used in teaching counselor skills, a didactic thrust, teaching counselors about case planning and management (called strategies in this book) should be a second major part of the counselor training program. Counselor trainees need to learn to identify appropriate ways to help clients set goals for counseling and ways to introduce effective behavioral styles for accomplishing these objectives.

To do this, trainees need instruction in the analysis of client behaviors. Counselors should acquire skill in specifying crucial antecedents and maintainers of client behaviors. Furthermore, they need to learn to identify and specify client behaviors that need to be changed and those which need to be acquired. Finally, they need to learn the relationship between the techniques and strategies they apply and the outcomes that are achieved. The ability to analyze the client's environment and behaviors, as explained in Chapter 3 and illustrated in the cases in Part II, must be developed. The counselor trainee must learn to see himself as an agent of change as well as, and possibly instead of, a "nice" person who relates well to a wide range of people. Prospective counselors generally seem to be attracted to the profession from the ranks of people who like to work closely with others and whose interpersonal relationships have been effective and satisfying to them. To this dimension of counselor attributes, training should add some skill in understanding behavior and its antecedents, in methods of bringing about changes, and develop a willingness to attempt to do so.

Counselor supervision. The behavioral approach to counseling suggests a number of implications regarding supervision. Of course, supervision is an advanced aspect of training; the neophyte counselor moves from the role of being closely scrutinized by his mentors to working relatively independently, using his judgment about when to consult a supervisor. The supervisory role played with each type of trainee thus varies. Generally, however, five kinds of supervisory functions seem evident. First is the continuing effort to impart a real and practical understanding of ethics, both of the "traditional" kind as represented by the APA or APGA ethical guides, as well as the ethics of involvement or non-involvement. In casework, live examples of ethical questions arise and have great impact on the trainee. These instances should be used as the locus of teaching an understanding of ethics.

Certain basic counseling skills should be taught by the supervisor, possibly through some adaptation of the method demonstrated by Ivey and his co-workers (1968). Basic skills in attending, eliciting information, analyzing environmental and behavioral information, etc., seem essential for the new counselor to acquire if he is to become skillful in identifying the proper approach to recommend to a client. Where one treatment is provided for all client problems the task of the counselor is relatively simple; he exhibits his skill (Callis, 1960) and either assumes or hopes that it will benefit the client. Where a "differential counseling" process is followed, however, the counselor has the responsibility to choose his procedure on the basis of characteristics and problems, and thus he needs to become skillful in client eliciting, noting, and analyzing the relevant information from the client.

The third and fourth supervisor functions are corollaries of the second. The supervisor must be sure the trainee is familiar with concepts about human behavior under different conditions. This means that the trainee must be familiar with personality, counseling and learning theory. In addition, the supervisor should expose the trainee to a wide range of counseling techniques which the neophyte can eventually modify and develop a facility in using. As a result, the counselor trainee should gradually acquire an "armamentarium" of counseling techniques from which he can draw as needed to implement strategies in various cases.

Finally, the supervisory function should include the provision of specific behavioral feedback to the trainee regarding his counseling skills. Since much of this feedback can be provided by means of video-tape recordings, the supervisor's role should emphasize the evaluation of the trainee's counseling behaviors as they are related to both the identification and implementation of counseling objectives.

Consulting. The behavior change counselor can approach the consulting task in a somewhat different manner than the insight counselor. Often the psychological consultant sees selected cases himself, or discusses subjective aspects of those cases with those directly involved with the troubled individuals. The cases are usually difficult ones usually unresponsive to treatment. The behavior change consultant can be more appropriately concerned with setting up conditions to perform a thorough environmental analysis. He might perform the analysis himself or he might develop guidelines and specifications for environmental analysis to be implemented by someone locally. The consultant would also work toward the identification of institutional programming to be introduced or changed.

On a more individual level, the consultant might contribute his services toward the behavioral assessment of clients exhibiting particularly complex or difficult behaviors. At the same time as his involvement in these individual cases would serve to help the clients, it would also serve as a model toward which local professionals might strive.

A final consultative role to be played includes the development and structuring of counseling routines, programs, or case management plans to be executed by subprofessional counselors, possibly technicians or even laymen. Some of the highly cognitive-interventionistic case strategies lend themselves well to the development of structured counseling programs. These highly structured programs might easily be implemented by people with little high level counseling training. For example, a knowledgeable study skills technician might be able to do an excellent job working with a restricted academic problem that had been assessed by a higher level professional. Similarly, a relaxation or desensitization specialist should require little high level training outside his specialty, provided cases referred to him were carefully screened. Migler and Wolpe (1967) have experimented with automated desensitization with some success, indicating that the consultant might be farther removed from the client than tradition assumes.

Counseling and institutional change

Since the interventionistic-cognitive approach includes techniques that go beyond the usual counseling interview, the approach naturally leads to considerations of environmental change. Obviously, the context in which behavior occurs strongly influences the behavior itself (e.g., the work of Astin, 1965; Pace and Stern, 1958). Thus, if one observes a high frequency of disruption in a particular population, two treatment strategies may be considered. One would apply intervention techniques to the afflicted individuals, the other would identify ways the environment had contributed to the disruption and lead to institutional modifications. For example, many colleges have long been accused of negligence in not graduating a high enough proportion of their entering students. Individually oriented solutions to the problem emphasize the development of counseling centers, reading and study improvement programs, educational-vocational counseling, etc. Institutions focus upon programmatic changes in curriculum, admissions, and large scale counseling interventions.

To carry the educational example further, one of the major environmental deterrents to scholastic effectiveness has been noted to be premature educational commitment without the possibility of a reasonable degree of reversibility. Thus, in a rigid institution a student might inappropriately begin his college studies in engineering, do poorly his first quarter or two and realize then that his talents and interests suggest he be enrolled in a different program. Upon realizing that, however, he may be unable to make the transfer because of the poor record he accumulated in engineering. As a result, he can choose between leaving school entirely, or remaining in engineering and either flunking out or performing marginally in an inappropriate program. Students who get a second opportunity to correct development errors can often go on to become productive and effective individuals.[1]

Besides identifying and striving to eliminate environmental deterrents, counselors can also work toward the identification of environmental facilitators. Much personal misery can be eliminated when student choice of program is reappraised in the light of current information about the student and the institution in which he is about to enroll. A program devised to help students obtain a current appraisal of their talents, personal inclinations, and institutional routes to various career pathways offered at the time of college entrance on a programmatic basis can be helpful in eliminating or moderating much of the educational disruption that is evident in higher education. Where such programs have been introduced the result has been a considerable revision of student plans, which is generally viewed by the students as helpful (Osipow, 1969). Obviously where used, such programs

1. The counseling program at the Pennsylvania State University illustrates the operation of such a program.

must be tailored to the local institution in order to be effective, and many variations and innovations are possible.

IMPLICATIONS FOR CASE MANAGEMENT

A number of changes of emphasis in clinical counseling are likely to result from the adoption of a behavioral-differential counseling approach.

Group counseling. The behaviorally oriented group counselor is logically concerned with two basic functions. First, he focuses the attention of the group on the importance of understanding the impact of the environment on their behavior. The counselor would teach his group techniques of environmental and behavioral analysis so that points of environmental leverage could be identified into which the group members would effectively introduce new behaviors.

Once that was accomplished, the group's tasks would emphasize the acquisition of new behaviors, new interpersonal skills, and the use of the group to provide feedback, opportunity for practice, and the reinforcement of newly acquired behaviors. Behaviorally structured groups would be task oriented, and unlikely to strive to elicit suppressed emotionality from their members. Rather, the objective of such groups is to teach its members the identification of realistic goals, the identification of personal and environmental barriers, and how these barriers may be overcome.

Case evaluation. When detailed behavioral objectives are specified in advance, each counseling case becomes a miniature experiment where hypotheses about client objectives, the means to accomplish them behaviorally, and methods of counselor intervention can be rigorously evaluated, because success in counseling is determined by individually tailored, specific behavioral outcomes. Does the shy client engage in more external interpersonal behaviors? Does the poor student exhibit more (and better) academic responses? Notice that the goals are not grand and vague. Asking "does the client have more friends" or whether the client feels better about his social interactions, are questions that are not operational enough for most clients to answer.

The use of behavioral goals does not preclude the introduction of sets of limited behavioral outcomes. A subgoal might be developed in working with a given client, which, when achieved, might lead to a new set of subgoals or case termination, depending upon what seems suitable to the client and the counselor. A client whose newly acquired social skills allow him to feel at ease with his peers might wish to reconsider his career objectives in the light of his new interpersonal satisfaction and competence.

IMPLICATIONS FOR RESEARCH

A great many new research directions are possible as a result of the change in emphasis growing from the application of the interventionistic-cognitive approach. One fundamental research stream to be expanded is the identification of syndromes of behavior. What behaviors are associated with which other behaviors, and what, if any, common antecedents do they share? For one thing, such data would permit counselors to take conceptual shortcuts in the analysis of behaviors and environmental antecedents. Secondly, the identification of behavior syndromes would not only make clusters of behavior amenable to change with increased efficiency, but would also allow the introduction of agents designed to change a whole set of related behaviors rather than merely one brief response sequence.

A second obvious research avenue is the development of new, and the improvement of old, techniques to foster behavioral and environmental analysis. These might include both psychometrically based instruments as well as new methods of the observation of behavior, by counselors or their aides.

Third, it is clear that, to be effective, new counseling techniques need to be developed. These go beyond the behaviors to be followed in the interview, and should include experimentation with variations in the scheduling and timing of counseling interviews. For example, why are counseling interviews tied so closely to the psychoanalytic model of weekly sessions of fifty minutes? "Demi" interviews rather than marathon or fifty minute sessions, may really be more suitable to deal with certain kinds of client difficulties. For example, frequent, brief interviews may be exactly what is necessary for successful performance-improvement counseling. Research is necessary to investigate such questions sensibly and take them out of the realm of speculation. Similarly, one might ask if it is necessary to restrict counseling techniques to the verbal realm, or if counseling must always take place in an office. Obviously not, but efforts need to be made both to devise and test new methods and to ascertain their feasibility and effectiveness with various kinds of clientele.

Finally, research efforts into the interaction between various kinds of counseling techniques and client characteristics seems to be in order. Some studies illustrative of a promising line of inquiry have already been done. Gilbreath (1967) has investigated two types of counseling with two kinds of academic underachievers. Bell (1970) has examined the differential effects of group-centered versus leader-centered counseling on the educational-vocational information seeking and decision making behavior of dependent and independent clients. Osterhouse (1969) studied the differential effects of two types of counseling (study skills versus relaxation and desensitization) on two types of test-anxious students. Once basic relationships between counseling approaches and client characteristics are established, more complex experimental designs covering a broader range of problems in more subjective situations can be produced. Only in this way can counseling effectiveness advance, gradually becoming more precise in its procedures.

SUMMARY

Some of the broad implications of the interventionistic-cognitive approach to counseling have been reviewed in this chapter. The IC view has impact on ethical questions, counselor selection, training, supervision, and consulting. the IC approach also leads to implications for institutional change and improved case management. While many of the implications cited are speculative, the approach suggests many productive avenues for research to validate or refute its efficacy. As Krumboltz (1966b) has stated, counseling may well be on the threshold of a revolution, a revolution leading to tremendous social relevance and impact.

REFERENCES

Allen, T. W., Whiteley, J. M., Sprinthall, N. A., Mosher, R., and Donagby, R. *Dimensions of effective counseling.* Columbus, Ohio: Merrill, 1968.

Ayllon, T. and Azrin, N. *The token economy.* New York: Appleton-Century-Crofts, 1968.

Astin, A. W. Effects of different college environments on the vocational choices of high aptitude students. *Journal of Educational Psychology*, 1965, *12*, 28-34.

Bell, G. The effect of interaction between client personality and counseling approach on vocational planning behavior. Unpublished Doctoral Dissertation, Ohio State University, 1970.

Callis, R. Toward an integrated theory of counseling. *Journal of College Student Personnel*, 1960, *1*, 2-9.

Carkhuff, R. R., Kratochvil, D., and Friel, T. Effects of professional training: communication and discrimination of facilitative conditions. *Journal of Counseling Psychology*, 1968, *15*, 68-74.

Cottle, W. C. and Lewis, W. W., Jr. Personality characteristics of counselors: II. Male counselor responses to the MMPI and GZTS. *Journal of Counseling Psychology*, 1954, *1*, 27-30.

Cottle, W. C., Lewis, W. W., Jr., and Penney, M. M. Personal characteristics of counselors: III. An experimental scale. *Journal of Counseling Psychology*, 1954, *1*, 74-77.

Gilbreath, S. H. Group counseling, dependence, and college male under-achievement. *Journal of Counseling Psychology*, 1967, *14*, 449-453.

Guilford, J. P. *The nature of human intelligence*, New York: McGraw-Hill, 1967.

Ivey, A. E., Normington, Cheryl J., Miller, C. D., Morrill, W. H., and Haase, R. F. Microcounseling and attending behavior: an approach to prepracticum counseling training. *Journal of Counseling Psychology Monograph*, 1968, *15*, 1-12.

Krumboltz, J. D. Behavioral goals for counseling. *Journal of Counseling Psychology*, 1966, *13*, 153-159 (a).

Krumboltz, J. D. Promoting adaptive behavior. In Krumboltz, J. D. (Ed.), *Revolution in counseling.* Boston: Houghton-Mifflin, 1966 (b).

Latané, B. and Darley, J. M. *The unresponsive by-stander,—Why doesn't he help?* New York: Appleton-Century-Crofts, 1970.

Migler, B. and Wolpe, J. Automated self-desensitization: a case report. *Behavior Research and Therapy*, 1967, *5*, 133-135.

Osipow, S. H. Student appraisal of a freshman preregistration counseling program. *Journal of College Student Personnel*, 1969, *10*, 47-51.

Osipow, S. H. and Walsh, W. B. Social intelligence and counselor selection. Unpublished data, Dept. Psychology, Ohio State University, 1970.

Osterhouse, R. A. A comparison of desensitization and study skills training in the treatment of two kinds of test anxious students. Unpublished doctoral dissertation, The Ohio State University, 1969.

Pace, C. R. and Stern, G. G. An approach to the measurement of psychological characteristics of college environments. *Journal of Educational Psychology*, 1958, *49*, 269-277.

Name Index

Subject Index

Adjective Check List, 51
affective counseling, 17–19
avoidance responses, 44

behavioral analysis, 37–53
  of biological and physical attributes
    46–47
  and counseling, 42–47
  and counseling strategies, 52
  of development stage, 42
  dimensions of, 41–42
  of educational environment, 41
  of family environment, 41, 45–46
  functional type of, 37–40
  of interpersonal environment, 46
  of motivational state, 42
  of neighborhood, 41
  of occupational environment, 41
  of problem, 43–44
  of problem situation, 41, 44
  of self-controlling behaviors, 42
  of social relationships, 42
  of social-cultural-physical
    environment, 42
  of thinking process, 46
  topographic type of, 37–40
  of work environment, 44–45
  behavioral appropriateness, 43
behavioral appropriateness, 43
behavioral assessment,
  illustrations of use:
    in behavior modification-acquisition
      case, 74–75, 110–112
    in behavior modification and
      decision making case, 102–103,
      115–116, 119–120
    in behavior modification-acquisition
      and supportive case, 84–86
    in performance type case, 97–99

    in performance and behavior
      acquisition type case, 91–93
    in supportive case, 78–80, 106–108
  physiological implications of, case
    illustration of, 87–90
behavioral data, methods for the
  collection of, 47–52
behavioral duration, 43
behavioral frequency, 43
  as baseline for outcome criteria, 40
behavioral goals, in behavior-
  modification-acquisition counseling, 62
behavioral intensity, 43
behavioral maintainence, 29–30
  role of aversive stimuli in, 38–39
  role of positive reinforcers in, 38–39
behavioral origination, 29–30
behavioral sequences, 33–34
behavioral syndromes, 33–34
Bernreuter Self-Sufficiency Scale, 48

cognitive counseling, 17–19
coping behavior deficit, 43–46
coping behavior excess, 43–46
coping responses, 43
counseling, as learning process, 11
  behavioral goals for, 30–31
  definition of, 9–13
  developmental framework for, 13–16
  diagnosis in, 23–37
    and interventionistic-cognitive
      theory, 24–25
    medical model for, 23
    methods for accomplishment of,
      26–34
    modern views of, 25–26
    role of antecedents in, 27–28
    role of situation in, 28–29
    various approaches to, 23–34